Insights into Chinese Culture

中国文化读本（英文版）

作者／**Authors:**

    叶　朗 (Ye Lang)

    朱良志 (Zhu Liangzhi)

译者／**Translators:**

    章思英 (Zhang Siying)

    陈海燕 (Chen Haiyan)

英文审订／**English Consultants:**

    May Yee（加拿大）

    Krisantha Sri Bhaggiyadatta（加拿大）

外语教学与研究出版社

FOREIGN LANGUAGE TEACHING AND RESEARCH PRESS

北京　BEIJING

图书在版编目（CIP）数据

中国文化读本 = Insights into Chinese Culture：英文版 / 叶朗，朱良志著
.—北京：外语教学与研究出版社，2008. 6
ISBN 978 – 7 – 5600 – 7635 – 5

I. 中… II. ①叶… ②朱… III. 文化—中国—英文 IV. G12

中国版本图书馆CIP数据核字（2008）第094623号

出 版 人：于春迟
责任编辑：时　娜
装帧设计：蔡　曼
出版发行：外语教学与研究出版社
社　　址：北京市西三环北路19号（100089）
网　　址：http://www.fltrp.com
印　　刷：北京雅昌彩色印刷有限公司
开　　本：787×1092　1/16
印　　张：17.25
版　　次：2008年6月第1版　2008年6月第1次印刷
书　　号：ISBN 978 – 7 – 5600 – 7635 – 5
定　　价：98.00元
＊　　＊　　＊
如有印刷、装订质量问题出版社负责调换
制售盗版必究　举报查实奖励
版权保护办公室举报电话：(010)88817519
物料号：176350001

Preface

The 2008 Summer Olympics in Beijing, with athletes and visitors attending from 205 countries and regions, will be the largest ever Olympic Games in history.

Since the dawning of the 21st century, the international community has been paying greater attention to China. People around the world want to learn more about Chinese culture in more comprehensive and profound ways. The Beijing Olympics will provide just such an opportunity. Friends from all parts of the world will savor the 5,000-year-long culture of this country and see what modern China is really like today.

It is at such a hopeful time that Professors Ye Lang and Zhu Liangzhi have written this book to share with readers their insights into Chinese culture.

Several years ago, Professor Ye Lang and I became friends when we worked together in initiating aesthetic education programs for children and youth, in an effort to improve their overall qualifications. Professor Ye is an influential philosopher and aesthetics scholar in contemporary China. In 2002 and 2003, he concurrently served as the dean for three departments at Peking University: Philosophy, Religious Studies, and Arts. Professor Zhu has long been engaged in research in Chinese philosophy and arts, with his special focus on Zen Buddhism, painting, calligraphy, and landscape gardening.

Beyond general knowledge, this book provides a detailed, vivid introduction to certain unique features and highlights of Chinese culture. The authors have attempted to represent the spirit and core values of Chinese culture, especially those with universal significance. They have also tried to exemplify the inner world, the life views and aesthetic interests of the Chinese people. They hope this book will serve as a popular introduction to Chinese culture for readers both in China and abroad. At the same time, they also hope their insights can provide a new perspective for readers to gain a deeper understanding of the true essence of Chinese culture.

Subjects covered in his book range from ancient wonders such as the Forbidden City, the Great Wall, the Terracotta Army, and traditional residences of ordinary people, to enduring artworks of calligraphy, painting, landscape gardening, Peking Opera, and porcelain. Under the authors' pen, these subjects have all been imbued with a living spirit to epitomize Chinese people's real life interests. Even in a game of go, the authors have discovered "kindred friendship" among the players, who play a "good game" through principles of cooperation and coexistence. In the description and analysis of *A Riverside Scene at Qingming Festival*, or of Old Beijing and Old Shanghai, the authors provide readers with glimpses of Chinese people's contentment with a peaceful and harmonious life. This is perhaps part of the reason why Chinese culture has lasted for thousands of years.

Not only is the text written in a superbly fluent and fascinating way, the accompanying illustrations also bring to life the splendor of many aspects of Chinese culture.

The publication of *Insights into Chinese Culture* is a timely addition to the content of the "People's Olympics."

李岚清

Li Lanqing
Vice Premier of China from 1993 to 2003

Contents

Art and Aesthetics

The Beauty of a "Virtual World"
"Watching a Play Is Watching Famous Actors"
Mei Lanfang, Great Peking Opera Artist

Cloisonné: Artifacts with the Gleam of Precious Gems
New Year Pictures: Enhancing the Festive Atmosphere
Papercuts: a World Created with Scissors
Embroidery: Ten Fingers Like a Spring Breeze
Shadow Play: the Art of Light and Shadow

Folk Customs

A Horizontal Scroll of the Scenery along the Bianhe River
Urban Civilization of the Northern Song Dynasty

Food in Old Beijing
Alleys and Hawkers' Cries
Bustling Tianqiao
Temple Fairs in Old Beijing
Leisure Life in Old Beijing

The Most Open City
Fashion Seekers
Shikumen and the Customs of the Alleys

Graceful Tang-style Fashion
Beautiful Cheongsam
Natural Wax Printing
Splendid Stage Costumes

Wisdom and Beliefs

Human beings have only one home under the heavens. How we arrange our domestic lives and how we live together in harmony is the essence of traditional Chinese thinking. First and foremost, Chinese culture regards human life as part of nature and, as such, the only way for us to survive is to live in harmony with nature. The fundamental significance of civilization lies in the creation of a peaceful world, which also requires avoiding conflict between humans and nature. Instead of dictating to nature, people should hold nature in awe and gratitude. A second characteristic of Chinese culture is its emphasis on harmonious human relationships. An individual cannot live without community and society. Thus Chinese culture strives to build a world of harmony based on friendship between individuals, mutual assistance between families, and respect between nations. Thirdly, Chinese thinking stresses self-reflection. People should not only understand the external world, but also and more importantly, improve their internal state of mind. Only after humans have cleared away any intentions of combating nature, are we able to live up to the philosophy of living in harmony with nature.

1. Confucian Thought on Heaven and Humanity

Confucius (551-479 BC), known in China as Kongzi, given name Qiu and alias Zhongni, was a native of Zouyi (present-day Qufu in Shandong Province) of the State of Lu during the Spring and Autumn Period (770-476 BC). A great thinker, educator and founder of Confucianism, Confucius is an ancient sage to the Chinese people. His words and life story were recorded by his disciples and their students in *The Analects (Lunyu)*.

An enduring classic of Chinese culture, *The Analects* has influenced all thinkers, writers and politicians in the over-2,000-year-long history of China after Confucius. No scholar could truly understand this long-standing culture or the inner world of the ancient Chinese without this book.

Much of Confucian thought on Heaven and people represent universal human values. This is perhaps why Confucian thought in the 21st century still retains the interest of not only the Chinese but also people in other parts of the world.

Confucius on Heaven: the Source of Everything

In the Shang (1600-1046 BC) and Zhou (1046-256 BC) dynasties, the prevalent concept of "Heaven" was that of a personified god, which influenced Confucius. Generally, however, Confucius regarded "Heaven" as nature. He said, "Heaven does not speak in words. It speaks through the rotation of the four seasons and the growth of all living things." Obviously, Heaven equaled nature, in the eyes of Confucius. Moreover, nature was not a lifeless mechanism separate from humans; instead, it was the great world of life and the process of creation of life. Human life was part and parcel of nature as a whole.

Confucius' equation of Heaven with the creation of life was an innovative idea in his time. The natural process of life creation was the "way of Heaven." This idea was later developed in *The Book of Changes* (*Yijing*), as it stated "Continuous creation of life is change."

As the natural process of creation of life, Heaven was the source of all living things and the source of all values. This was the "virtue of Heaven." Thus, *The Book of Changes* said, "The great virtue of Heaven and Earth is creating life."

In the natural process of creation of life, Heaven had its inner purpose in creating all things as well as protecting and improving life. Heaven had originated humanity, and humans were obliged to accomplish this purpose. In other words, humans are born with a sense of "heavenly mission," and this is the meaning of human life.

Confucian "Heaven" also had a certain sacred element, which was related to it being the source of life. Thus Confucius required people to hold Heaven in awe. He says that a person of virtue must "respect his heavenly mission," listen to and live out the purpose of Heaven by caring for and improving life.

Under the influence of Confucius, the ancient Chinese developed a sense of awe and belief in Heaven. To them, Heaven was the highest sacred being, with its profound mystery never to be fully understood by mortals. It was not a supernatural, personified deity, but was the world of ever-generating life. As the most intelligent of all beings, humans should take to heart the purpose of Heaven by cherishing life. If one remained "ignorant and disrespectful of one's heavenly mission" by killing or maiming life, one would be punished by Heaven. Confucius said, "He who offends against Heaven has none to whom he can pray." The Confucian respect for and belief in Heaven represented a form of religious spiritualism of the ancient Chinese.

In the 21st century, the Confucian caveat of "standing in awe of the ordinances of Heaven" still holds true, as human society begins to pay greater attention to ecological civilization. Humans should indeed listen to the voice of nature, respecting and loving it as the world of life. This is our sacred mission and gives value to all human life.

Confucius on People: *ren* (仁) and *li* (礼)

Ren and *li* are the two core concepts of Confucius' doctrine about people.

When his student Fan Chi asked him about *ren*, Confucius replied, "Love of people." This is Confucius' most important interpretation of *ren*. Love for the people is universal love. Confucius further emphasized that this kind of love should "begin with the love of one's parents." He believed no one could love people in general if they did not even love their own parents. Confucius regarded "filial piety and fraternal duty" as the essence of *ren*. *The Doctrine of the Mean (Zhongyong)* quotes Confucius as saying, "The greatest love for people is the love of one's parents." He also said, "Children should not travel far while their parents are alive. If they have no choice but to do so, they must retain some restraint." He did not mean that children should not leave their parents at all. What he meant was that children should not make their parents anxious about them while away from home. Confucius said again, "Children should think often of the age of their parents. They should feel happy for the health and longevity of their parents. They should also feel concern for the aging of their parents."

Cry of Deer in a Red Maple Forest
(detail), unknown artist, Song Dynasty, a
scene of contentment and harmony, as
valued by Confucian scholars

By *ren*, Confucius meant universal love based on love of one's parents. How should people love one another then? Confucius said, "One should be aware that other people may have similar desires as oneself. While fulfilling one's desires, allow others to fulfill their desires as well." He further said, "Do not do toward others anything you would not want to be done to you." Thus from oneself to one's family, from family to society, one should extend love to all people. Mencius (c. 372-289 BC), a great Confucian scholar, best summarized *ren* as, "loving one's parents, loving the people, loving everything in the world."

Today, the Confucian doctrine of "Do not do toward others anything you would not want to be done to you" still holds true for humankind.

Li refers to rituals, traditions and norms in social life. Of these, Confucius regarded burial rituals and ancestral worship rituals as the most important, because they arose from human feelings. He said, "A child should not leave his parents' bosom until he is three years old." He naturally loved his parents.

The ritual of wearing mourning for a deceased parent for three years was an expression of the child's love and remembrance.

Confucius placed emphasis on *li* with the aim of preserving social order, stability and harmony. *The Analects* says, "The role of *li* is to maintain harmony among people."

Li also has philosophical implications. While individuals have a limited lifespan, life in nature is everlasting. Life is given by one's parents and extended through one's children. In this way, a limited, individual life becomes merged with the limitless life of nature; the individual dream of eternal life can thus come true. Through burial rituals and ancestral worship rituals, people are able to experience the everlasting continuity of life, appreciating the value and meaning of life. This gives people metaphorical solace.

Confucius on the State of Life

Before Confucius, only the nobility had the right to education. He was the first figure in Chinese history to initiate private education. According to historical records, Confucius taught for many years and trained 3,000 disciples. A total of 72 of them excelled in the "six arts," i.e., ritual, music, archery, (carriage) driving, calligraphy, and mathematics. A great educator, Confucius has been admired by later generations as the "sage of sages."

Confucius believed the basic goal of education was to cultivate "persons of virtue," who should have sound character and uplifted minds. Such persons should be able to shoulder important social responsibilities and to make contributions to society. Confucius regarded lofty ideals, great virtue, love of people, and the "six arts" as the general principles of education. Of these, virtue was the most important. His students were involved in a variety of professions, including politics, trade, education, diplomacy, ritual ceremony, and classifying ancient books. Whatever they did, they all wanted to improve their learning of the humanities and to enhance their virtue.

Three Masters Smiling beside Tiger Stream, *unknown artist, Song Dynasty. Buddhist master Huiyuan (334-416), of the Eastern Jin Dynasty, bids farewell to two honored visitors at sunset – Confucian scholar and poet Tao Yuanming (c. 365-427), and Daoist high priest Lu Jingzhi (birth and death dates unknown). They are smiling as they walk along, though they have crossed Tiger Stream without knowing it. Huiyuan has thus broken his own rule of not seeing guests off across Tiger Stream.*

Confucius emphasized aesthetic education. He said, "Studying *The Book of Songs (Shijing)* inspires the spirit and helps one appreciate beauty. Studying *The Book of Rites (Zhouli)* enables one to behave properly as a person of enlightenment. Studying music lifts the spirit and helps one to enjoy life." He also said, "Simply knowing the highest standard of virtue (i.e., love of people) is not as good as setting it as one's goal. Setting it as one's goal is not as good as enjoying the practice of it."

On one occasion, Confucius asked several of his disciples to talk about their aspirations. Zi Lu and Ran You wanted the opportunity to administer a state. Gongsun Chi wanted to become a master of rituals. Zeng Dian said, "My aspiration is different from theirs." "That is acceptable," said Confucius. "We are only talking about our own aspirations." Zeng Dian then said, "(My dream)

論語卷之一

學而第一

朱熹集註

此為書之首篇，故所記多務本之意，乃入道之門，積德之基，學者之先務也。凡十六章。

子曰：「學而時習之，不亦說乎？

說，悅同。○學之為言效也。人性皆善，而覺有先後，後覺者必效先覺之所為，乃可以明善而復其初也。習，鳥數飛也。學之不已，如鳥數飛也。說，喜意也。既學而又時時習之，則所學者熟，而中心喜說，其進自不能已矣。程子曰：「習，重習也。時復思繹，浹洽於中，則說也。」又曰：「學者將以行之也。時習之，則所學者在我，故說。」謝氏曰：「時習者，無時而不習。坐如尸，坐時習也；立如齊，立時習也。」

有朋自遠方來，不亦樂

樂，音洛。○朋，同類也。自遠方來，則近者可知。程子曰：「以善及人，而信從者眾，故可樂。」又曰：「說在心，樂主發散在外。」

乎？

人不知而不慍，不亦君子乎？」

慍，紆問反。○慍，含怒意。君子，成德之名。尹氏曰：「學在己，知不知在人，何慍之有？」程子曰：「雖樂於及人，不見是而無悶，乃所謂君子。」愚謂：及人而樂者順而易，不知而不慍者逆而難，故惟成德者能之。然德之所以成，亦曰學之正、習之熟、說之深，而不已焉耳。○程子曰：「樂由說而後得，非樂不足以語君子。」

有子曰：

「其為人也孝弟，而好犯上者，鮮矣；不好犯上，而好作亂者，未之有也。君子務本，本立而道生。孝弟也者，

弟、好，皆去聲。鮮，上聲，下同。○有子，孔子弟子，名若。善事父母為孝，善事兄長為弟。犯上，謂干犯在上之人。鮮，少也。作亂，則為悖逆爭鬥之事矣。此言人能孝弟，則其心和順，少好犯上，必不好作亂也。

其為仁之本與！」

與，平聲。○務，專力也。本，猶根也。仁者，愛之理，心之德也。為仁，猶曰行仁。與者，疑辭，謙退不敢質言也。言君子凡事專用力於根本，根本既立，則其道自生。若上文所謂孝弟，乃是為仁之本，學者務此，則仁道自此而生也。○程子曰：「孝弟，順德也，故不好犯上，豈復有逆理亂常之事。德有本，本立則其道充大。孝弟行於家，而後仁愛及於物，所謂親親而仁民也。故為仁以孝弟為本。論性，則以仁為孝弟之本。」或問：「孝弟為仁之本，此是由孝弟可以至仁否？」曰：「非也。謂行仁自孝弟始，孝弟是仁之一事。謂之行仁之本則可，謂是仁之本則不可。蓋仁是性也，孝弟是用也，性中只有箇仁、義、禮、智四者而已，曷嘗有孝弟來。然仁主於愛，愛莫大於愛親，故曰：『孝弟也者，其為仁之本與！』」

子曰：「巧言令色，鮮矣仁！」

巧、令，皆好也。好其言，善其色，致飾於外，務以悅人，則人欲肆而本心之德亡矣。聖人辭不迫切，專言鮮，則絕無可知，學者所當深戒也。○程子曰：「知巧言令色之非仁，則知仁矣。」

曾子曰：「吾日三省吾身：為人謀而不忠

省，悉井反。為，去聲。三，傳，並平聲。○曾子，孔子弟子，名參，字子輿。盡己之謂忠。以實之謂信。傳，謂受之於師。習，謂熟之於己。曾子以此三者日省其身，有則改之，無則加勉，其自治誠切如此，可謂得為學之本矣。而三者之序，則又以忠信為傳習之本也。尹氏曰：「曾子守約，故動必求諸身。」謝氏曰：「諸子之學，皆出於聖人，其後愈遠而愈失其真。獨曾子之學，專用心於內，故傳之無弊，觀於子思、孟子可見矣。惜乎！其嘉言善行，不盡傳於世也。其幸存而未泯者，學者其可不盡心乎！」

乎？與朋友交而不信乎？傳不習乎？」

子曰：「道千乘之國：敬事而信，節用而愛人，使民以時。」

道，乘，皆去聲。○道，治也。千乘，諸侯之國，其地可出兵

A page from The Analects, *with annotations by Zhu Xi (1130-1200), a great Confucian scholar of the Song Dynasty* is to wear spring robes in late spring and to swim in the Yi River with five or six adults and six or seven children. We shall enjoy the breeze where people pray for rain. Then we shall go home, singing all the way." Confucius sighed, "Ah, I share Dian's aspiration." The different aspirations of the four students reflected their different outlooks on life. Confucius' agreement with Zeng Dian indicates that while he stressed individual contribution to society, he regarded the highest state of life as harmony among people and harmony between people and nature. His was a true aesthetic outlook on life.

Under the influence of Confucius, Chinese thinkers of later generations all believed that students and scholars should not only increase their knowledge, but also and more importantly, broaden their minds and enhance their spiritual ethos. In other words, they should continually seek the greater meaning and value of life. Many modern scholars think the theory on the perspective on life is the most valuable feature of Chinese philosophy. It all began with Confucius.

Hanbi Pavillion in Jichang Garden, Wuxi, Jiangsu Province. "Hanbi" means "encompassing green," representing the Confucian ideal of keeping one's mind open and inclusive.

2. Laozi's Philosophy of Non-action

The book *Laozi* was written around the sixth century BC. The author is generally believed to be Lao Dan, or Laozi – a recluse who lived during the Spring and Autumn Period (770-476 BC). Few records have survived about Lao Dan, who was said to have once held a low civil position in the royal court, in charge of the archival records of the Zhou Dynasty (1046-256 BC). Yet, due to his great learning, even Confucius was said to have traveled miles to consult him.

Laozi (Laozi), also known as *Classic of the Way and Virtue* (*Dao de jing*), consists of just over 5,000 Chinese characters. Its 81 chapters are divided into two parts, *Dao* (the Way) and *De* (Virtue). Short as it is, the book has played a tremendous role in the development of Chinese culture. It became the basis of Daoism, the school of philosophy parallel to Confucianism in ancient China. The thought of Laozi formed the foundation of Daoism, the most influential indigenous school of religion in China. It has also exerted a direct impact on the characteristics, trends of thought and aesthetic sensibilities of the Chinese nation. Today *Laozi* still plays a role in the development of Chinese thinking.

Laozi was first introduced into Europe possibly as early as the 15th century and has been one of the most translated philosophical works of ancient China. Many of Laozi's enlightening views are based on his philosophy of naturalness and non-action.

Naturalness and Non-action

"Naturalness" is an important concept of Laozi's philosophy. It refers to a natural state of being, an attitude of following the way of nature. Laozi emphasized that everything in the world has its own way of being and development: birds fly in the sky, fish swim in the water, clouds float in the sky, flowers bloom and flowers fall. All these phenomena occur independently and naturally without following any human will, and humans should not try to change anything natural. Laozi admonished people to give up on any desire to control the world. Following the way of nature is the way to resolving conflicts between humans and the world.

"Non-action" is another important concept of Laozi's philosophy. It is the guarantee of "naturalness." Laozi said, "(*Dao* or the Way) acts through non-action," by which he did not mean that one should do nothing and passively wait for something to be achieved. Neither did he deny human creativity. What he meant is that human enterprises should be built on the basis of naturalness, not on any attempts to interrupt the rhythm of nature. Human creativity should be in compliance with the ways of nature.

Laozi said, "Great ingenuity appears to be stupidity." This is the essence of "naturalness" and "non-action." "Great ingenuity" refers to the highest level of ingenuity, arising so naturally that it does not resemble ingenuity at all. Ingenuity can be achieved through human effort, but "great ingenuity" is superior to ordinary ingenuity. To Laozi, resorting to deceit is true futility and would accomplish just the opposite result. Those who intend to play tricks are not genuine and therefore are not natural. Deceit is detrimental to naturalness and to the harmony of life.

Zhuangzi (369-286 BC), the philosopher who carried on Laozi's philosophy, had the following story to tell about a "useless tree":

A carpenter went with his apprentice to the State of Qi. On the way they came across a giant tree by the local temple for the deity of the earth. Its trunk was several dozen meters thick and as tall as a mountain. Its branches could provide shade to several thousand cattle. While people thronged to worship the super tree, the carpenter passed it without taking a look. The apprentice, however, was fascinated. After carefully studying the tree, he ran to catch up with his master and asked, "Ever since I became your apprentice, I have never seen such fine wood. But you just kept walking without even looking at it. Why?" The master replied, "That tree produces useless wood. If you made a boat out of it, the boat would sink. If you made a coffin out of it, the coffin would soon rot. If you made utensils out of it, they would wear out quickly. Its wood is of no use at all. That is why this tree has been able to live so long." The wisdom of the "useless tree" lies exactly in its uselessness, or its naturalness.

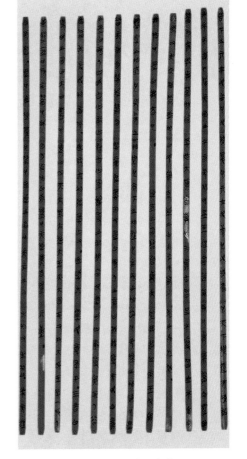

Bamboo strips inscribed with the text of Laozi, unearthed in Guodian, Hubei Province. These bamboo strips were buried in the tomb of an aristocrat of the State of Chu, c. 300 BC. This is the earliest version of Laozi discovered so far.

The Philosophy of Non-contention

On the basis of "naturalness" and "non-action," Laozi proposed the view of "overcoming the strong by being weak." The era Laozi lived

渾而為一其上不皦其下
微此三者不可致詰故復
闡名曰希搏之不得名曰
視之不見名曰夷聽之不
身為天下若可託天下
為天下若可寄天下愛以
無身吾有何患故貴以身
有大患者為吾有身及吾
何謂貴大患若身吾所以
失之若驚是謂寵辱若驚
為寵辱寵為下得之若驚
寵辱若驚貴大患若身何
不為目故去彼取此
令人行妨是以聖人為腹
獵令人心發狂難得之貨
馳五味令人口爽馳騁田
五色令人目盲五音令人耳
之以為利無之以為用

Calligraphy from Laozi *by the Yuan-dynasty calligrapher Xianyu Shu (1246-1302)*

in was replete with endless wars. Therefore, war was an important theme for philosophers, and anti-war thinking was the norm. Even the great strategist Sunzi advocated "winning a war without fighting it," not to mention the great thinker Confucius, who strongly championed a government based on love. Their contemporary Mozi (c. 468-376 BC), founder of Mohism, also condemned wars while calling for "love for all."

According to Laozi, war springs from humanity's bloated desires. Conflict arises out of people's struggles to satisfy their desires, and conflict escalates into war. Therefore, Laozi's philosophy is based on "non-contention." To him, human striving and competitive strife is the root cause of decline; desiring nothing is the natural way of life.

Laozi said, "The greatest virtue is like water." He compared his philosophy of "non-contention" to water, to distinguish it from the law of the jungle. He said, "Water nourishes everything but contends for nothing." To Laozi, humans tend to seek higher positions while water always flows to lower places. Driven by desire, humans like whatever they think is superior while despising whatever they think is inferior. Yet water always flows downward. As the source of life, water nourishes all living things on Earth. No life can exist without water. Water contributes to the world without regard for gain or loss. Remaining low, level and tranquil, water embraces and reflects everything under heaven. The way of water is completely different from the way of people with avid desires.

But the philosophy of Laozi is by no means weak. On the contrary, it is full of strength. According to Laozi, water accumulates great strength in its weakness and quietude. Its strength can break down all barriers in the world. He said, "Nothing in the world is weaker than water. Yet nothing is stronger than water when it comes to breaking something strong." Water is a typical example of the weak winning over the strong. Water is invincible because it desires nothing and contends for nothing.

A corner of Geyuan Garden in Yangzhou, Jiangsu Province. The landscape embodies the concept of naturalness in Daoist philosophy.

Laozi said, "Aware of the strong, one should remain weak." This does not mean that Laozi promoted failure. To become strong, however, one must not oppress the weak. Instead, one should start with one's own weak points, accumulating strength by keeping low, just as water does. Giving up the desire to flaunt one's superiority is the basic way to prosperity.

Remaining weak is not only the way to prosperity, but also the way to preserving life. Laozi regarded fragility as the symbol of life. He explained this with a comparison between life and death: when a person is alive, his body is fragile; when he dies, his body becomes hard and rigid. The same is true with plants: living plants have supple leaves and lovely flowers, while dead plants become dry and hard. Laozi uses these examples to show that the way of the weak is the way to preserving life. The way of the weak is the best way to avoid conflict.

Returning to a Newborn State

Laozi saw the world as a madding crowd of vanity. He chose to live a simple, quiet life, and to keep his mind undisturbed in the face of temptation. He said he would rather remain a "newborn baby."

This does not mean Laozi wanted to remain childishly ignorant. He believed that sages – people with the highest virtue – all resembled newborns. The highest level of one's cultivation was to return to the state of a newborn baby.

The state of the newborn is free of any knowledge, desire, impurity or falsehood. Laozi's state of the newborn refers to "complete innocence." The first cry of a baby when it leaves the mother's womb is pure and clear, which, according to Laozi, is the call of genuine life.

When human beings come into the world, they gradually acquire external knowledge and accept social norms, along with the growth of their bodies. Step by step, their originally pure minds become tainted with chaotic colors.

As humans mature, they become more and more hypocritical. The process of acculturation is the process of losing one's true self.

To Laozi, civilization is to a certain degree a departure from the "true self." The development of human culture is a process of "decoration": clothing as decoration of the body, houses as decoration of the way of living, language as decoration of communication, and state politics as decoration of human organization.

Such "decorations" often turn into bloated desires. Desire-driven, human beings fight and deceive one another, leading to war. Laozi made a comparison between the laws of nature and the laws of the human world. Nature takes from the surplus to make up the deficit, such as the wind leveling sand dunes and the water washing away earth and stones. The human world is just the opposite, i.e., robbing the poor and oppressing the weak.

Bloated desire has damaged the external world as well as poisoned the human mind. Laozi said, "Beautiful colors blind the eyes, complex music harms the ears, rich flavors numb taste, while riding and hunting madden the mind." Desire disturbs peace of mind. If immersed in a sea of desire, in the end humans would be submerged.

3. Sunzi's Art of War: Source for All Books on War

Sunzi's Art of War (*Sunzi bingfa*), is an ancient classic on war. It consists of 13 chapters in about 6,000 characters. Sun Wu, respectfully called Sunzi, was born sometime between 550 and 540 BC, or toward the end of the Spring and Autumn Period (770-476 BC). He was a native of the State of Qi but later moved to the State of Wu, where he became the king's trusted strategist. As many of the book's contents bear features of the Warring States Period (475-221BC), some scholars believe the book was probably written in the middle of that period. It represents the theories of war of the Sunzi School originated by Sun Wu.

Of the more than 3,000 books on war from the pre-Qin (before 221 BC) period to the Qing Dynasty (1616-1911), *Sunzi's Art of War* stands out as the greatest classic. It excels over the other books in terms of strategy design, philosophical grounding and in tactical application. Over the centuries it has been respected as "the source for all books on war."

The Strategic Thoughts of Sunzi

Of the rich strategic thoughts of Sunzi, we have selected just a few for illustration.

The first example is, "Planning before going to war." Before entering a war, one must compare and analyze all factors of both sides. These mainly include: morale, climate, terrain, commanders, and rules. "Morale" refers to the approval or disapproval of the people. The army that has the approval of the people will gain their support, while one without endorsement will lose their support. "Climate" refers to seasonal conditions at the time of war. "Terrain" refers to the distance (far or near), position (ease or difficulty of access), size (large or small), and height (high or low) of the topography for war. Consideration must also be given to the degree of security or danger in the area. "Rules" refer to regulations governing the army, "Who should carry out orders? What are the respective strengths of the soldiers? Who is responsible for training the troops? Who decides rewards or punishments?" The five aspects for consideration during war were echoed by Carl von Clausewitz (1780-1831), a German war expert, as "strategic factors." One or two of these factors are insufficient for one to judge the feasibility and consequences of a war. Consideration must be given to all these factors and their combinations. Such holistic thinking is a special feature of *Sunzi's Art of War*.

The second example is, "One can fight and win a hundred wars if one knows both oneself and the enemy." This is probably the most widely quoted concept from *Sunzi's Art of War*.

The purpose of considering the five aspects, as introduced above, is actually to know the real situations on both sides. It is not easy to get to know the enemy, because they do their best to keep their secrets and resort to all sorts of deception. Getting to know oneself is not easy, either. What do the people think about the war? What is the capability and state of mind of the commander? How is the morale and training of the troops? These factors are not usually self-evident without thorough analysis, and one may be misled by false impressions. There have been more than a few cases in history where the commander received permission from the ruler to go to war, but without reporting to him that the army was in fact incapable of fighting. The result, needless to say, was always total destruction of the army. This is why Sunzi said, "One can fight and win a hundred wars if one knows both oneself and the enemy. The odds for winning are half and half if one knows oneself but not the enemy. And one is bound to fail if one knows neither oneself nor the enemy." He added, "The odds for winning are half and half if one knows that one's troops are able to attack but does not know the enemy troops are invulnerable to attack. The odds for winning are half and half if one knows that the enemy troops are vulnerable to attack but does not know that one's own troops are not in a position to attack. The odds for winning are half and half if one knows that the opponent is vulnerable to attack and that one's troops are in a position to attack but does not know that the terrain is unsuitable for fighting. Thus an expert of war does not leave anything unclear when declaring war, and also has all sorts of methods to deal with any situation. Victory is certain, if one knows both oneself and the enemy; victory will be complete, if one further knows seasonal and topographic conditions."

The third example, "The army survives by treachery." Sunzi said, "The use of force is actually the use of treachery." In his discussion of "strategy" in *On War*, Carl von Clausewitz attributes its origin to "treachery."

By "treachery" Sunzi meant that the army "should appear to be incompetent when it is competent, appear to be unprepared to fight when it is prepared, appear to be retreating when it is advancing, appear to be advancing when it is retreating." In other words, it is crucial to deceive the enemy with false impressions.

By treachery, one should "tempt the enemy with gains, attack the enemy when they are in disorder, be prepared for the enemy when they are equal in strength, avoid the enemy when they are stronger, (further) aggravate the enemy when they are angry, cause the enemy to become arrogant when they are prudent, tire the enemy when they are at rest, sow discord among the enemy when they are united." In a word, treachery is meant to entice the enemy to make all sorts of mistakes, defeating them after they fall into a state of chaos. It also means "attacking the enemy at an unexpected time and place."

It is by using treachery that an expert of war devises strategies at headquarters while directing his army a thousand miles away to victory.

The fourth example is, "Winning a war without fighting it." Sunzi did not approve of large-scale killing and destruction, which he regarded as the worst strategy. To Sunzi, the purpose of a war is to win victory, not to kill as many people as possible. On the contrary, one should avoid destroying the enemy stronghold and avoid destruction of life as much as possible. It is best to take over a city intact and to win victory through minimal killing. This is the principle of a "decent victory." Sunzi went on to say, "Winning every war one fights is not the best one can do; winning a war without fighting is the best one can do. Therefore, the highest art of war is to outwit the enemy strategically, the second level is to foil their diplomacy, the third level is to attack their army, and the lowest level is to attack their city. Attacking the city can only be used as the last resort." In other words, it is not plausible to fight and win wars. It is ideal to achieve victory through means other than war, such as politics, diplomacy, and other deterrent measures. Attacking the city is the least preferable, because,

Bamboo strips inscribed with the text of Sunzi's Art of War. Discovered buried in a tomb from early Western Han Dynasty on Mount Yinque, in today's Shandong Province, this is the earliest version of the book discovered so far.

especially in Sunzi's time, the city was host to many ancestral temples and tombs. The defensive side would often fight to their death, resulting in extensive casualties and destruction. These ideas of Sunzi reflect his deep understanding of what we today call "holistic war."

The Dialectical Thinking of Sunzi

The rich philosophical thought in *Sunzi's Art of War* has aroused greater and greater attention from scholars of ancient Chinese philosophy.

Situations of war are changeable at every moment, perhaps the most changeable of all things in the world. To win a war, the commander must be able to keep abreast of and adapt to such changes. Sunzi said, "There is no fixed way of using force, just as there is no fixed form to water. He who can win a victory by adapting to changes in enemy forces is a master of the art of war." Sunzi draws special attention to the changing dynamics in the opposite direction, saying, "Chaos compares with order, cowardice with bravery, and weakness with strength." These contrasting situations may change into their opposites. Thus, it is not uncommon for an army to turn failure into victory or vice versa. Sunzi reminded commanders to consider gains and losses from both positive and negative sides. He said, "Some routes can be taken but should not be, some enemy troops are vulnerable but should not be attacked, some enemy cities can be captured but should not be, and some enemy territory can be obtained but should not be." This is a warning to commanders to be aware not only of potential gains but also of potential losses. Sunzi further advised commanders, "Do not intercept the enemy on their retreat to their home country, leave a gap when besieging the enemy, and do not approach a desperate enemy." In other words, Sunzi was against going beyond the limits in military operations, because things would turn into their opposites once they reached their extreme.

In analyzing changes in opposing factors in war, Sunzi also emphasized pushing them into their opposites for the benefit of one's own troops. He said, "When we know the enemy situation but they do not know ours, we can keep our troops together while they have to keep them separate. Now that our troops are in one place while the enemy troops are dispersed in ten places, we can strike them with tenfold force. In this way, our troops enjoy an absolute majority while the enemy suffers an absolute minority." *Sunzi's Art of War* is full of such dialectical thinking. Sunzi said, "By taking a tortuous route deliberately while tempting the enemy with small gains, we can arrive earlier despite having started later than the enemy. This is the strategy of turning a tortuous route into a straight one." As a kind of synopsis, Sunzi said, "The expert commander is able to make the enemy follow his direction, not the other way round."

Sunzi's Cautions Against War

As a military classic, *Sunzi's Art of War* provides a complete set of strategies and tactics for winning a war. Paradoxically, the book does not encourage rulers to be bellicose but rather warns them again and again to refrain from waging a war without careful consideration.

At the very beginning, the book points out, "The use of force is a matter of life or death for the soldiers, the people and the country." Such a matter can never be taken lightly. At the end of the book, Sunzi raised the warning once more, "A head of state must not wage a war spurred by a momentary anger, and the commander and general must not wage a war spurred by a momentary bad mood. They must take into consideration overall national interests for declaring war or desisting from war. Anger can turn into delight and a bad mood can change into a good mood, but a country lost is lost forever and those killed are dead forever. Therefore, a wise ruler must handle matters of war with extreme care, and good commanders and generals must handle them with the greatest caution as well. This is the cardinal principle for safeguarding the country and the army."

Sunzi's cautions against war were continued in *Sun Bin's Art of War (Sun Bin bingfa)*, by a strategist in the middle of the Warring States Period. While teaching military professionals how to fight and win wars, Sun Bin (birth and death dates unknown) also cautioned that, fighting and winning every war is not a good thing; those who are bellicose and intent on winning victory through wars are bound to fail and only bring shame on themselves.

Sunzi's Art of War and *Sun Bin's Art of War* both warn readers of the great dangers of war. Such thoughts represent, as great strategists, their concern and care for human life. As nuclear war looms larger in today's world, the cautions of Sunzi and Sun Bin certainly deserve the serious attention of those who have the power to push "the button."

Sunzi's Wisdom Beyond the Military

Sunzi's Art of War was introduced abroad from the Tang Dynasty (618-907) onwards. A Japanese student named Kibimakibi took the book home in 734 or 752. It was introduced to Korea in the 15th century during the Joseon Dynasty. Up to the 17th century, more than 170 books on the study of *Sunzi's Art of War* were published in Japan. In 1772, Jean-Joseph-Marie Amiot (1718-1793), a Jesuit missionary from France, published in Paris his French translation of the book. That year, Napoleon Bonaparte I (1769-1821) was only three years old. A Russian translation was published in 1860. Later translations of the book include English, German, Italian, Czech, Vietnamese, Hebrew, and Romanian.

After World War II, famous strategists and scholars from different countries took a new interest in *Sunzi's Art of War*. Bernard Law Montgomery (1887-1976), British field marshal during that war, declared that all military

The Fanyang sword, a weapon widespread in the late Warring States Period, unearthed in Luoyang, Henan Province

academies in the world should include the book as required course material. New translations and more research works on the book have been published since that time.

With the spread of *Sunzi's Art of War*, its influence has gone beyond the military to many other fields, including economics, politics, culture, and diplomacy. Many people regard the book not only as a military work, but also as a work on the philosophy of strategy, referring to the application of military strategies as general methods and principles in all areas of social life. In 2001, online bookseller Amazon listed the book as one of the bestsellers in the humanities category. Many contemporary scholars regard Sunzi's wisdom to be as universal as Confucius' wisdom.

4. The Temple of Heaven: Reverence with Awe and Gratitude

The Temple of Heaven was constructed during the reign of Emperor Yongle (r.1403-1424) of the Ming Dynasty (1368-1644), and completed in 1420, about the same time as the Forbidden City. When Emperor Yongle moved the capital from Nanjing to Beijing in 1420, it was at the Temple of Heaven that he performed the important ritual of paying tribute to Heaven and Earth.

Nearly 600 years later, the Temple of Heaven still stands intact in the south of Beijing. Covering an area nearly four times as large as the Forbidden City, the Temple of Heaven, with its numerous halls and buildings, attracts visitors from around the world. It not only presents a beautiful spectacle, but also represents the Chinese pursuit of harmony between Heaven and mortals.

*The Temple of
Heaven after a
snowfall – a sight of
divine purity*

Ceremonial Offerings of the Emperor

The emperor used to offer oblations to Heaven here twice a year, in the spring and winter. The Hall of Prayer for Good Harvests was the site of the spring rituals, where the emperor and the ministers would gather for the ceremony signified by the name of the hall. On the Winter Solstice, they would make offerings at the Circular Mound Altar, to show their gratitude for the great compassion of Heaven toward the human world. In times of drought or flood, the emperor would come here with civil and military officials to pray for assistance from heaven.

Only the emperor could pray at the Temple of Heaven. Ordinary people were not allowed access. Yet the idea of showing awe and respect to Heaven was not reserved for the emperor alone, but was shared by the people as well.

The worship of Heaven among the Chinese dates back to over 3,000 years ago. Our ancestors believed that Heaven, also known as the "Heavenly Deity" or "Heavenly Emperor," was the mysterious force that directed all things on Earth, such as natural harvests and personal fate. Heaven stood for righteousness. Natural disasters on Earth were regarded as warnings to people for wrongdoings of one kind or another. In the face of a calamity, people would say, "This is punishment from Heaven." In the second year of the reign of

Emperor Guangxu (r. 1875-1908), the Hall of Prayer for Good Harvests was burned down in a big fire. The emperor lost his composure at the news and all the ministers turned ashen gray, believing the disaster to be a bad omen from Heaven. To the ancient Chinese, however, Heaven was more inclined toward love and tolerance, punishing people only occasionally. Thus, our forebears were always grateful to Heaven.

Holding Nature in Awe

The architecture of the buildings in the Temple of Heaven ingeniously embodies the concept of holding nature in awe. While blue is the thematic color, the three main structures of the Temple of Heaven all stand on triple-terraced white foundations. The colors used invoke a strong sense of purity and sublimity—qualities the Chinese attribute to Heaven.

A bird's-eye-view of the Circular Mound Altar

The Hall of Prayer for Good Harvests

The Temple of Heaven is supposed to be close to Heaven. Careful visitors will notice the centripetal structures of the two main buildings, the Circular Mound Altar and the Hall of Prayer for Good Harvests. This type of architecture gives one a sense of reaching up to Heaven while ascending the steps.

The Circular Mound Altar, as its name suggests, is a round structure with three tiers. When you ascend the steps to the altar, no matter from which of the four directions, you find yourself entering a centripetal world. On the top tier, you find a round stone at the center surrounded by circle after circle of blue flagstones fanning out. The round stone represents the heart of Heaven and is aptly called "Heavenly Heart Stone." The tablet representing Heaven was placed on this stone when the emperor offered oblations on the Winter Solstice.

The process of approaching the Heavenly Heart Stone represents the process of approaching Heaven. The Circular Mound Altar has no physical roof, but is covered only by the boundless sky.

Humanity and Heaven in Communion

Ancient Chinese believed that people could communicate with Heaven, and the Temple of Heaven was built to enable this. The echo of sound at the Circular Mound Altar and the Imperial Vault of Heaven are evidence of what our forebears believed to be communicating with Heaven.

If you stand on the Heavenly Heart Stone on the Circular Mound Altar, you can hear your voice rise from underneath your feet and echo back from the wall around the Altar. The resounding echo, according to the designers, represents Heaven's reply to whatever the speaker asks for.

When you stand inside the outer wall of the Imperial Vault of Heaven, and speak into the wall, a friend at a point farther away along the wall can hear your voice; it resembles making a phone call to someone. This phenomenon, due to the much shorter length of the sound waves compared to the radius of the round wall, gave rise to the nickname "echo wall" for the outer rim of the Vault.

5. Eco-awareness in Traditional Chinese Culture

Protection of the eco-environment is capturing wider international attention today. Eco-ethics and eco-philosophy have arisen in the face of the increasingly serious ecological crisis facing the whole world. Scholars in the field point out that human damage to the natural environment has accelerated to such an extent as to threaten the very existence of human beings themselves.

The main idea of eco-ethics and eco-philosophy is to replace "human-centrism" with "eco-holism," which means that all living things in the earth's biosphere are entitled to equal rights similar to those of human beings, or the rights to survival and development.

When we examine traditional Chinese culture, we also find from ancient times a strong eco-consciousness that is at one with eco-ethics and eco-philosophy.

The Philosophy of "Life"

Traditional Chinese philosophy is a philosophy of "life." To Confucius, Heaven is the source of all living things. He regards the "creation of life" as the "Heavenly Way" and the "Heavenly Destination." *The Book of Changes (Yijing)*, following Confucius' viewpoint, explains, "The continuous creation of life is change," and "The great virtue of Heaven and Earth is creating life." Mencius (c. 372-289 BC), a great Confucian scholar who lived just over 100 years after Confucius, said, "(One should) love one's family, love the people, and love all living things in the world." Confucian thinkers of later generations carried on the idea of "Heaven and Earth giving birth to all life," and thus emphasized love for and kindness toward all living things. For example, many prominent

Slender West Lake in Yangzhou, Jiangsu Province, a scene of vibrant life

Confucian scholars of the Song Dynasty (960-1279) echoed their master's view on life. Zhou Dunyi (1017-1073) said, "Heaven creates life through *yang* and nurtures life through *yin*." Cheng Yi (1033-1107) said, "The nature of life is love." Zhang Zai (1020-1077) said, "All people in the world are my brothers and all beings in the world are my companions." Cheng Hao (1032-1085) said, "Those with love regard themselves as the same as other living things in the world." We can see from their thoughts that Confucian love starts from loving one's family and other people, to loving all living things in the world. Humans and other living things are of the same kind and are equal with each other.

In a letter to his family, Zheng Banqiao (1693-1765), a great painter of the Qing Dynasty (1616-1911), wrote that he loved all living things in the world, be it an ant or an insect. This, he said, was the "will of Heaven," and that human beings should understand Heaven's will. He was strongly opposed to "keeping birds in a cage," saying, "It is unreasonable to keep them in a cage just to please myself, to oppress their nature to suit my nature!" Even ferocious animals like wolves and

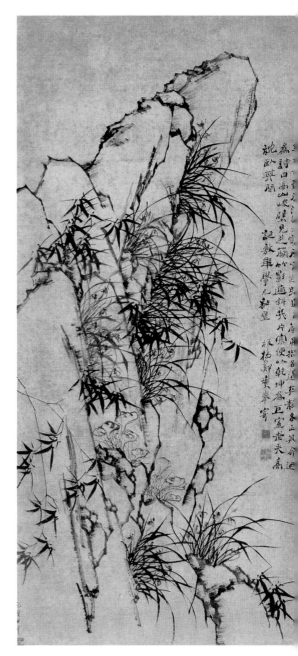

Orchids on Rocks, *by Zheng Banqiao (1693-1765), Qing Dynasty. The painting is of a pure and lively style.*

Dragonfly and Lotus Flower,
by Qi Baishi (1864-1957).
The painting represents the
artist's focus on an innocent
yet vivid style.

tigers should only be driven away so they cannot harm people. People have no right to kill them at will. He went on to say that, if people really love birds, they should plant more trees as their home. When people rise in the morning and hear the birds singing, both would be happy. He described such a happy scene as, "(All living things) each live by their respective nature." Only in this way could human beings share real happiness with their fellow beings.

Ecological Aesthetics

Related to eco-ethics and eco-philosophy is the eco-aesthetics of traditional Chinese culture.

Ancient Chinese thinkers regarded nature, with human beings included in it, as the world of life. All living things in the world have their own life and state of being. "Life and its state of being is most worthy of appreciation," said Cheng Hao. From such appreciation, people could draw the greatest spiritual delight, according to such philosophers. Confucian scholars in the Song and Ming dynasties all enjoyed observing "the state of being of living things." Zhou Dunyi, for example, allowed the grass to grow in front of his window without cutting it. When asked why, he explained that the natural growth of grass was in line with his idea of living things. He "observed the creation of life and the state of being of living things in the world" through the grass. The state of being of the grass was similar to the state of being of people, and the experience of this resemblance gave him great pleasure. Cheng Hao "felt great joy from observing living things." He would often appreciate the fish he kept, and enjoyed watching newly hatched chicks. To him, the lively and lovely chicks best represented the "state of being."

Humans at One with Other Living Things

Love for all living things in the world and appreciation for their state of being can often be found in ancient works of art and literature.

Dong Qichang (1555-1636), a famous painter of the late Ming Dynasty, explained that, most artists enjoyed a long life because everything they observed was full of life. Dong You (birth and death dates unknown), collector and connoisseur of the Song Dynasty, emphasized that artists should depict the state

A detail from a wall of the Canglang Pavilion in Suzhou, Jiangsu Province. The flying eaves of the pavilion, like the wings of a bird, impart a sense of motion, an aesthetic ideal in Chinese architecture.

A detail from a wall of the Canglang Pavilion in Suzhou, Jiangsu Province. The green leaves of Japanese banana trees strikingly set off the white wall.

of life, which exists in nature. Therefore, artists should observe and learn from nature. Wang Gai (1654-1710) of the Qing Dynasty summarized the secret of painting fish as: depicting their liveliness as they swim in water. He compared the happiness of fish in their natural world to the happiness of humans in their natural world. Chinese artists never paint dead animals. The birds, fish, insects, and flowers are all full of vitality under their brush.

Ancient Chinese literature has a similar focus. In the poems of the Tang and Song dynasties, when Chinese poetry reached the apex of development, birds and flowers were often depicted as if they had human feelings. In *Strange Tales from Make-do Studio* (*Liaozhai zhiyi*), by Pu Songling (1640-1715), human beings and other living things are described as being of the same kind. Many of the stories tell of love between men and beautiful women incarnated from plants or animals. "Xiangyu" is such a story. The heroines, Xiangyu and Jiangxue, are incarnated from, respectively, a peony flower and a camellia flower in a monastery on Mount Laoshan (sacred mountain of Daoism). Xiangyu falls in love with Huang Sheng, a scholar studying at the monastery. Jiangxue also becomes his friend. Unfortunately, a visitor to the monastery grows so fond of the white peony flower that he moves the plant to his home, where it withers up. The heartbroken Huang Sheng composes 50 poems entitled *Crying over the Flower*. Then the priests of the monastery want to cut down the camellia plant in order to build extra rooms there, but Huang Sheng stops them. Later, a new plant sprouts from where the white peony used to be. In his sleep, Huang Sheng dreams of Xiangyu begging him to water her every day. He follows her request. The plant grows more luxuriant day after day. The next year a large flower blooms, on which sits a tiny beauty. In a blink of the eye, the beauty floats onto the ground. She is none other than Xiangyu. The three of them live happily together. Later, Huang Sheng falls seriously ill. He leaves this message to an

Waterside in Tuisi Garden, Suzhou, Jiangsu Province. This landscape design represents an idyllic scene of "hawks circling above and fish diving below," an ideal aspired to in Chinese philosophy.

old priest, "You will find a red sprout growing vibrantly from underneath the white peony. It will grow into five leaves. That's me." The year after Huang Sheng's death, a plump sprout indeed appears. The old priest diligently waters it. The sprout grows over three years to become a plant more than a meter tall, but it does not blossom. After the old priest dies, his disciple cuts down the plant because it never flowers. Soon afterward, the white peony plant dies, immediately followed by the death of the camellia plant.

"Xiangyu," like many other tales by Pu Songling, is full of love for all living things in the world. These stories are to signify that humans and other living things are of the same kind, and they share weal and woe together.

Creativity and Exchange

Over a history of 5,000 years, Chinese people have produced numerous inventions. These include traditional Chinese medicine, silk, porcelain, the compass, paper, printing, and gunpowder. Some ancient landmarks also bear witness to Chinese people's creativity, such as the Great Wall and the Forbidden City.

At the same time, the Chinese people have always kept an open heart toward friends and cultures from other lands. The prosperity of the Tang Dynasty (618-907), for example, was largely due to Emperor Taizong's (r. 627-649) open attitude toward the outside world. In the early Ming Dynasty (1368-1644), Emperor Yongle (r. 1403-1424) sent envoys to the Western Seas on seven long voyages. They reached as far as Mecca in West Asia and Mozambique in Africa. Wherever the Chinese travelers went, they carried out material and cultural exchanges under the principle of spreading peace.

6. Chinese Characters: Poetic Symbols

The numbers of Chinese language learners across the world have been on the rise in recent years. While those used to phonetic languages often find Chinese characters difficult to learn, some learners may experience the gratification of discovering historical and cultural elements in the process.

Symbols of Sentiment

Some pictographic symbols of Chinese characters express people's keen observation and experience of the world. This is why some European poets have found Chinese characters inspiring to their imagination. Ezra Pound (1885-1972), for example, was well known for his admiration of Chinese characters, from which he was able to draw creativity. When he saw the character 旦 in the dictionary, he was reminded of the morning sun.

Pound's poetic allusions are not without basis. Take the character 旦, for example – the upper part is a sun symbol, while the lower part represents the horizon. In other words, the character indeed stands for "the sun rising on the horizon." The name of a famous university in Shanghai, Fudan, is composed of the characters 复 and 旦. Taken from a line from the classic, *Great Comments on the Book of Documents* (*Shangshu dazhuan*), meaning, "The sun and moon rise day after day," the characters were chosen to encourage students to learn new knowledge every day.

A number of characters containing 日 as an element all relate to the rising or setting of the sun. For example, the original complex form of the character for "east," 東, looks like the sun rising from a forest. One of the complex forms of the character for the "morning sun" is written as 朝. The left part consists of the symbols for "sun" and "grass." The right part is the symbol for "river." The

An oracle bone unearthed in Anyang, Henan Province

character means "the morning sun rising and shining over the flowing river." The character 暮 was originally written as 莫, resembling a scene of the sun setting into a forest. The left part of the character 明 was originally the symbol for "window," while the right part stands for "moon." Thus, 明 depicts a scene of the moon shining through the window. Is this not a poetic conception? The complex character for "beauty" is written as 麗. It resembles two deer running side by side on a mountain. A beautiful scene, is it not?

Graceful Olympic Symbols

The 2008 Olympics Games has adopted a set of symbols to represent the beauty of Chinese calligraphy. By combining certain features of different traditional forms of Chinese characters, the symbols appear both lively and highly representative of the sports they stand for.

Although Chinese is a pictographic language, it does not consist of language pictures. Early pictographic languages were mostly represented by language pictures, which imitated the external characteristics of things. For these languages, language symbols were not much different from pictures, as with the pictographic hieroglyphs of ancient Egypt.

A copy of stone-drum inscriptions, dating back to the Warring States Period, by Wu Changshuo (1844-1927), Qing Dynasty

Tomb tablet to Zhang Jing (official of unknown birth and death dates), inscribed with characters in official script, a style of calligraphy current in the Han Dynasty. This work later became one of the most popular models for students of calligraphy.

At its beginning, Chinese also included language pictures, which became fewer and fewer during the period of the oracle-bone inscriptions. Most symbols were made up of simple lines. For example, the oracle-bone inscription for "dog" was written as 犬. Instead of a drawing, a few simple yet highly symbolic lines were used to depict the image of a dog.

The calligraphic symbols for the Beijing Olympics were designed to represent the "Beauty of Seal Characters." A "seal character" is a type of Chinese calligraphy often carved on seals. There are two types of seal characters: the *dazhuan*, or greater seal, and the *xiaozhuan*, or lesser seal. The greater seal is also known as bronze inscription, because it was often used for carving inscriptions on bronzeware in ancient times. The lesser seal was the script the First Emperor of Qin (r. 246-210 BC) adopted for the whole country, when he united China in 221 BC. Based on and developed from the oracle-bone inscriptions, the seal characters feature smoother and rhythmic lines, and thus have a more appealing appearance.

This is the symbol for "swimming":

游 泳
Swimming

The upper part is a symbol for "person," while the lower part is a symbol for "water." The swimmer strokes the water with vigor, imparting a strong sense of motion. If we take a look at the seal character for "walk," 走, we make out a clear connection between the Olympic symbol and the character: the upper part for "swinging arms" and the lower part for "walking legs." The gentle and flowing lines in the lower part of the Olympic symbol are similar to the seal character for "water": 水.

This is the symbol for "track and field":

田 径
Athletics

This symbol is aptly taken from the seal character for "dance": 夨 . The dancer slightly tilts his head to one side, leans his body forward, swings his arms back and forth, and lifts his legs in a running fashion. The symbol, athletic yet graceful, has also been adopted for the "triathlon" and "football."

These symbols demonstrate how modern Olympics have revitalized the charm of the ancient Chinese language.

7. The Silk Road

The Silk Road refers to a transport route connecting ancient China with Central Asia, West Asia, Africa, and the European continent. It appeared as early as the second century and was traveled mainly by silk merchants. The term "Silk Road," or "*die Seidenstrasse*" in German, was first noted down by the German geographer Ferdinand von Richthofen at the end of the 19th century.

The Silk Road began in Chang'an (present-day Xi'an, capital of Shaanxi Province), passing through Gansu and Xinjiang to Central Asia, West Asia, and to lands by the Mediterranean. There were no signs of communication between ancient Chinese civilization and Mediterranean civilization in earlier history. In about the seventh century BC, the ancient Greeks began to learn about an ancient civilization to the east, yet knew little about it. Before the Silk Road, according to archeological findings, there had already existed an intermittent trade route on the grasslands from the Yellow River and Indus River drainage areas to the Euphrates and Tigris, and the Nile drainage areas. Yet real communication between China, Central and West Asian countries, Africa and the European continent did not develop until the opening of the Silk Road.

The Silk Road functioned not only as a trade route, but also as a bridge that linked the ancient civilizations of China, India, the Mesopotamian plains, Egypt, and Greece. It also helped to promote the exchange of science and technology between east and west. The Silk Road served as the main channel for ancient China to open up to the outside world, as well as for fresh impulses from other cultures to enter the country, which contributed a significant share to the shaping of Chinese culture.

Zhang Qian, Trail Blazer

The pioneer who blazed the trail of the Silk Road was Zhang Qian (c. 164-114 BC), a general of the Western Han Dynasty (206 BC-AD 25). In Zhang Qian's time, the Chinese had little knowledge about Central and West Asian countries, Africa or Europe, although they were aware of the existence of many different countries and cultures in faraway places to the west.

During the reign of Emperor Wu (r.140-87 BC), there were 36 small kingdoms in the Western Regions (present-day Xinjiang and parts of Central Asia). All of them were later conquered by the Huns, who then posed a direct threat to the Western Han and blocked the dynasty's path west. Under these circumstances, Emperor Wu appointed Zhang Qian to lead a team of more than 100 envoys to the Western Regions. The mission was to unite the Indo-Scythic people against the Huns, who once killed their chieftain. Zhang Qian's team set

Yongchang ("everlasting prosperity") brocade of the Eastern Han Dynasty, showing a high level of textile technology

out in 138 BC. No sooner had they entered the Hexi Corridor (northwest of present-day Gansu Province), when they were captured by the Huns. After being held under house arrest for over ten years, Zhang Qian and only one other remaining envoy managed to escape and return to Chang'an in 126 BC. Their accounts about the Western Regions were a revelation to the Han emperor and his ministers.

In the next two decades, Emperor Wu launched three major campaigns against the Huns, forcing them to retreat from the Western Regions. In 119 BC, the emperor sent Zhang Qian on a second mission to the Western Regions. This time Zhang Qian went further west, while his deputies reached more than a dozen countries in South and West Asia, and the Mediterranean.

Zhang Qian's two missions to the Western Regions opened up the road to the west. Emperor Wu adopted a series of measures to strengthen ties with the Western Regions, including encouraging Han people to trade there. Soon the route was bustling with caravans of camels carrying goods of all types and reverberating with the tinkling of their bells. Through the Silk Road, trade flourished between China and Central, South and West Asian countries, Africa, and Europe. In 166, envoys from Rome arrived via the Silk Road in Chang'an, where they set up an embassy.

Diamond-pattern embroidery of the Western Han Dynasty

The Silk Road also facilitated active trade between India, Southeast Asia, West Asia, Africa, and Europe. The exchange of new goods and technologies from different continents greatly helped to promote the development of all the civilizations involved.

Opening to the "West"

The Silk Road exerted an inestimable influence on the lives of the Chinese people. While Chinese culture and technology, such as papermaking and printing, were introduced to countries to the west, China also absorbed many elements from the arts, philosophy and religions of many other countries. This helped to promote an open policy toward other cultures from the Han to Tang dynasties.

The Silk Road highlights a period of history when China looked west for a farther vision of the world. To the east, apart from the islands of the Pacific and Japan, the country faced only a huge ocean. To the west, in contrast, there were many countries in the Western Regions and beyond. By the tenth century, Chinese explorers had already realized there were rich countries, attractive goods and artworks, and different peoples beyond the Western Regions. This aroused great interest in the "west" among ancient Chinese people.

Buddhism, for example, was first introduced to Khotan Kingdom (covering present-day Hetian

Bird-and-flower embroidery of the Northern Song Dynasty

area of Xin jiang) in the Western Regions in 87, and then gradually spread to the Central Plains along both the southern and northern routes of the Silk Road. This religion has since exerted a huge influence not only on Chinese beliefs but also on the development of Chinese thinking. Nestorianism and Islam were also introduced to China through the Silk Road.

Cultures and arts from other lands have left valuable legacies along the Silk Road, such as the murals in the Gaochang, Kuche and Dunhuang grottoes. They stand as evidence of a stunning blend of Chinese and western art and culture.

Shiva and Parvati

Murals in the Kuche Grottoes

As Buddhism spread east along the Silk Road, many large temples and grottoes were built in oases, housing exquisite statues and murals. Most of them have been destroyed or damaged over the centuries, yet some have survived, especially the murals in grottoes. Of these, the murals of the Qiuci Kingdom, covering today's Kuche area in Xinjiang, are some of the most remarkable.

While most of the grotto murals in Kuche depict Buddhist tales, a number of them attract special attention by representing a rich mix of the ancient cultures of China, India, Egypt, Greece, Mesopotamia, and Central Asia.

A mural in Niuche Cave, Kuche, Xinjiang

A mural in Mogui ("devil") Cave, Kuche, Xinjiang

Some paintings depict images of the Buddha with a bright aura emitting from his arms, legs and feet. Flying apsaras are seen playing all sorts of musical instruments, such as the pipa, panpipe and flute. The sun god sits on a two-wheeled chariot, and the golden-winged king of birds appears either as a two-headed eagle or an eagle with a human head. Seahorses with wings in flight and doves holding rings of flowers in their beaks bear a clear resemblance to Greek art.

Shiva, wearing a colorful robe, has three human heads, one animal head, and three hands. Parvati (also spelled Parvathi or Parvathy, a Hindu goddess and nominally the second consort of Shiva) sports earrings and beautiful jewelry on her head, arms and hands. Some frescos depict Persian kings and knights in helmets and suits of armor, and artists in Egyptian-style black wigs holding brushes and palettes in their hands.

Many pictures portray scenes of song and dance. Among the many musical instruments, ranging from those of China (panpipe and *ruanxian*, a plucked instrument), Persia (*pipa*, *suona*, a woodwind instrument, and the vertical *konghou*, a plucked instrument with five to 25 strings), India (bowed *konghou* and a five-stringed instrument), and Greece (*lila*, a plucked stringed instrument), are also seen a wide variety of flutes, horns and drums.

Dancers can be divided into solos and duets. Single male dancers usually sport long scarves, which fly in the air as the dancers swirl rapidly. Female soloists wear only capes and necklaces of pearls and jade on their naked bodies. Duets comprise a male and a female of different complexions. The male usually sports Buddhist robes and has his arm on the female's shoulders or around her neck in an intimate manner. The female wears a pair of pants with flared bottoms and plays a bowed *konghou* in a most feminine posture. Their bodies curve in an S shape, with both the male and female in a duet dance on half-tiptoes. The dancing style represents that of India and West Asia.

Most outstanding of the murals in Kuche are a large number of nude human images, especially of beautiful female bodies. These include many female acolytes listening to the Buddha espousing Buddhist teachings.

A mural in Yueshi ("musician") Cave, Kuche, Xinjiang

God of Heaven, a mural in one of the Kuche grottoes

Singing Goddess, a mural in one of the grottoes in Kuche, Xinjiang

Highlights are the female dancers with S-shape body contours, full breasts and round buttocks. These paintings show a clear influence of Indian and Greek art, especially Buddhist art from India.

A fine example is the mural depicting what scholars call "Mahamaya (mother of Gautama) bathing." The young lady, uncovered except for her private parts, stands crossed-legged under a tree with fire-shaped flowers. She sports a few flowing ribbons on her body and jewelry around her neck and wrists. Two maids are kneeling in front of her. Two other girls are walking towards the tree, each holding a jar of water on her shoulder. Their costumes have wave-like patterns with dark-yellow hems and their water jars evoke an ancient Greek style. The mural as a whole features both Greek and Indian artistic influences.

Another fresco bearing clear Greek and Indian connections has a king and his queen as subjects. The king, with a pale yellow complexion, sits cross-legged in the center. His wife sits on his right, resting her left hand on the king's shoulder. The queen wears assorted jewelry on her naked body, including three gold chains around her waist that tie into a knot in the front of her body. She wears snake-shaped leggings, and both she and the king wear earrings. The king has bright eyes and handsome features. He is holding the hand of a child, and a Buddhist monk is kneeling in front of him. A lady in Greek costume behind the child is speaking excitedly to the king. Two servants stand behind the king and queen, with their palms pressed together in Buddhist greeting.

The Kuche grotto murals represent a rich treasure-house left by the Silk Road. They are historical confirmation that the exchanges and integration of different civilizations bring forth the most brilliant flowers of art.

8. Openness of the Great Tang

The Analects (Lunyu) begins with the Confucian edict: "Is it not a pleasure to meet friends from afar?" "Afar" implies different ways of life and philosophies. Confucius' attitude shows that the Chinese have always highly respected friends from a long way off and aspired to learn from them. At the same time, there existed the wish to present a good image to outsiders. There is another useful quotation from *The Analects*: "Magistrate Zigao of the Ye County asked about governance. Confucius replied, 'Good governance makes one's neighbors happy and attracts people from faraway places to come and learn from you.'"

The prosperous Tang Dynasty (618-907) best exemplified the open and inclusive spirit of Chinese culture as advocated by Confucius. Instead of denial or confrontation, the Tang, from the reign of Emperor Taizong (r. 627-649) onwards, tolerated and absorbed elements from all cultures that it came into contact with, leading to prosperity in all aspects of social life.

Arts from All Corners of the World

Both the Tang and the preceding Sui Dynasty (581-618) presented large-scale song and dance performances at court banquets and ceremonies. The Sui had a nine-section musical symphony, and the Tang added one more section for such occasions. Besides Han music and Xinjiang regional music, both the nine-part and the ten-part musical works included elements from foreign cultures, including India, Burma and Cambodia. Love for music from other lands was prevalent not only among the imperial family and the nobility, but also among the common people. "Every household in Luoyang (secondary capital of the Tang) is eager to learn the music of diverse nationalities," vividly describes the atmosphere of that time. Musical instruments popular during the period include the pipa and *bili* (bamboo pipe with a reed mouthpiece, from Persia), and *konghou* (plucked instrument with five to 25 strings, from India). The horizontal flute was originally called a *qiang* flute. Originally from India, it had been introduced into northwest and southwest China, inhabited by the Qiang people, gradually evolving into today's form. *Melody on Splendid Fairy Costumes* is said to have been composed by Emperor Xuanzong (r. 712-756) after he paid a visit to the moon. Actually, the emperor had adapted the piece from the *Brahman Melody* of the Western Regions. Therefore, it can be regarded as the fruit of the harmonizing of the music of the Han and other nationalities.

Accompanying such music was also the different dances of diverse nationalities. "Swirling Dances" (from an area in today's Uzbekistan) and "Jumping

Tri-colored glazed pottery statue of a lady with a lovely smile, Tang Dynasty

Dances" (from near present-day Tashkent) were two of the most famous dance forms of the diverse peoples at the time. "Records of Rituals and Music," in *The New Chronicles of the Tang Dynasty* (*Xin Tangshu*), had this to say about "Swirling Dances": "The swirling dancer stands on a ball, swirling like the wind." Many poets of the time also left behind works on "Swirling Dances." The imperial court often put on shows of minority music and dance. Emperor Xuanzong himself was an excellent player of the flute and Jie (a branch of the Huns) drum. The court also attracted some outstanding artists, dancers, singers, and musicians from abroad.

Such an open attitude toward international arts was responsible for the flourishing of all forms of the arts during the Tang Dynasty.

Religious Diversity

Nestorianism, a branch of Christianity, was introduced into China during the reign of Emperor Taizong. Nestorius (c. 386-c. 451), the founder, was condemned for practicing heresy and expelled by the Roman Church in 431. He later died in exile in the deserts of western Egypt. His followers seceded from the Roman Church and started spreading their religion to the east. Olopen (birth and death dates unknown), one of their archbishops, arrived in Chang'an in 635 with his retinue, calling themselves "Nestorians." Emperor Taizong appointed Prime Minister Fang Xuanling (579-648) to welcome them and assigned the imperial library to them to translate their religious scriptures. The government even provided funds for the newcomers to build a church in the capital city.

Pottery statue of a female pipa player, Tang Dynasty

Two other religions, Zoroastrianism and Manichaeism, were also introduced into China during the Tang Dynasty. Zoroastrianism originated in Persia, where it was twice established as the state religion. It had been introduced by Suguda merchants entering China in the early 4th century, and was officially recognized in the early Tang Dynasty. Manichaeism had been created by Mani (216-c. 274), a Persian, later banished by the Zoroastrians. After Mani was persecuted to death by the Persian king Bahram I in 277, his followers fled abroad, spreading their religion to many other places. It has been documented that Manichaeism reached the inlands of China as early as the reign of Emperor Gaozong (r. 650-683). Empress Wu, who ruled the Tang Empire from 690 to 705, approved the teachings of Manichaeism as well.

Seeking Buddhist Truths

Not only did the Tang Empire open its doors to overseas friends and embrace foreign cultures, many of its people also went abroad to study local cultures. Xuanzang (602-664) and Yijing (635-713), both great Buddhist masters, were two of the most outstanding examples.

Xuanzang left China for South Asia in 627, and returned to Chang'an in 645. During those 17 years, he visited and studied Buddhism in more than 100 small states in the Western Regions and in and around what is now South Asia. He brought home 657 sets of Buddhist scriptures. Emperor Taizong met and conversed with Xuanzang for more than ten hours in Luoyang, and appointed more than 50 learned monks to help him translate the scriptures. Xuanzang worked as the chief translator and assigned different responsibilities to the other monks: some assisted him in translation, others checked the translations against the original Sanskrit, while some polished the finished translations, and so on. Xuanzang worked day and night over the next 19 years and translated 75 sets of scriptures in 1,335 volumes. He also dictated the 12-volume *Tang-dynasty Records of the Western Regions* (*Datang xiyu ji*), written down by his disciple Bianji (birth and death dates unknown). The book recounted what Xuanzang had experienced or heard about in the 138 countries or states in the Western Regions, including their geography, transport, climate, products, peoples, languages, history, religions, politics, economies, cultures, and customs. Contemporary scholars today regard the book as a rare reference for the study of South Asian history and philosophy, as well as religious and literary history.

Yijing also traveled to South Asia to study Buddhism, but he took the sea route. He left Guangzhou (capital of today's Guangdong Province) in 671, and traveled through Sumatra to arrive in India. He brought back 400 sets of Buddhist scriptures. Empress Wu came out of her palace to welcome Yijing with a splendid ceremony. Later Emperor Zhongzong (r. 705-710) set up a translation institute for Yijing at the Dajianfu Temple in Chang'an. As many as 83 translators worked for 16 years, to accomplish the translation of 56 scriptures in 230 volumes. These included 13 people from other lands, as well as 32 officials, of whom 11 were prime ministers. Such a large-scale and high-level translation

Song-and-music Performance at the Court, *by Zhou Fang (birth and death dates unknown), Tang Dynasty*

team is strong evidence of the Tang Empire's openness to foreign cultures.

Chang'an as an International Metropolis

The Tang capital Chang'an was probably the largest metropolis in the world at the time. It ran nearly 10,000 meters from east to west, and more than 8,000 meters from north to south. More than a million people lived in the 84-square-kilometer city, 200,000 more than the population of Constantinople, then capital of the Byzantine Empire.

Colored pottery of a man of minority origin, Tang Dynasty

Its open and inclusive attitude toward foreign cultures enabled Chang'an to develop into the most prosperous international metropolis in the world of the time. Foreign envoys, merchants, and students were a common sight in the city. The Honglu Temple received envoys from more than 70 countries, most coming in large groups. Japan, Silla (Korea), and Tazi (including today's Syria, Kuwait, Iraq, and Libya) were the countries that dispatched the largest numbers of envoys to China. Japan sent more than ten delegations of "envoys to the Tang," with delegates from all walks of life, including students, scholar-monks, craftspeople, and specialists in different fields. Every delegation consisted of several hundred people, the largest group numbering as many as 800. One to two hundred students from Silla studied regularly in Chang'an. According to *Old Records of the Tang Dynasty* (*Jiu tangshu*), in the year 837 there were 216 students from Silla in Chang'an.

Both aristocrats and the common people were keen on foreign apparel, foods and customs, with "Minority Folk Fashions" highly popular in Chang'an. "Minority Fashions" referred to

Tri-colored pottery of a camel carrying musicians, Tang Dynasty

attire from the Western Regions and some lands in what is today's Uzbekistan. They featured short jackets with narrow sleeves – convenient for traveling or hunting on horseback. The capes that Tang women enjoyed wearing were introduced from India. Polo, popular during the Tang, was originally a Persian sport. It was first introduced into Turkey and India, and then into China. It has been recorded in historical documents that Emperor Xuanzong and Emperor Xizong (r. 874-888) were great polo players. Many merchants from Central Asia and West Asia ran wine shops, jewelry shops, and sundry stores in Chang'an. Their wine shops attracted customers not only due to their famed wines but also because of the beautiful chorus girls from the Western Regions. It became vogue to patronize wine shops with these chorus girls. The great Tang poet Li Bai (701-762) wrote several poems on their beauty, such as: *"As beautiful as flowers, / The minority women smile like the spring breeze in the wine shops."* *"With nowhere to visit at the end of spring, /Smiling I enter a wine shop with women from other lands."*

These popular practices of adopting outside styles and customs represented the youthful dynamism of the Tang Dynasty, garnering high admiration from scholars of later generations.

9. Zheng He's Voyages to the Western Seas

On the 11th day of the 7th lunar month of 1405, a huge fleet of 208 ships appeared on the blue seas of the earth. With more than 27,500 people aboard, it was the greatest fleet with the largest crews the world had ever seen. Carrying cargoes of porcelain, silk, tea, and numerous other treasures, the fleet navigated the South China Sea, passing through the Strait of Malacca, and traversing the Indian Ocean to arrive at countries on the coasts of Asia and Africa. Over the next 28 years, six more fleets of a similar scale, with crews totaling more than 100,000 people, left China for further voyages to the Western Seas and arrived in more than 30 countries along the way – "Western Seas" being the term used in ancient China to refer to the regions west of the South China Sea. In West Asia, they visited the holy city of Mecca; in Africa, they reached as far as the port of Beira (in present-day Mozambique).

The commander of the fleet was Zheng He (1371-1433), an important official in the court of Emperor Yongle (r. 1403-1424) of the Ming Dynasty (1368-1644). Born to a Muslim family, Zheng He also believed in Buddhism and Mazu (Chinese goddess of the sea). Intelligent and knowledgeable about navigation, he was entrusted by the emperor to direct all seven adventurous missions.

Advanced Navigation Civilization

From the 15th century on, humans had accelerated their pace in combing the oceans. Christopher Columbus (1451-1506) came upon the continent of the Americas in 1492 by traveling across the Pacific with his Spanish fleet. The Portuguese fleet of Vasco da Gama (1460-1524) passed around Africa's Cape of Hope and across the Indian Ocean, to arrive at Calicut on the west coast of India in 1498. Ferdinand Magellan (1480-1521) and his Spanish fleet claimed the first round-the-world navigation in 1522.

Compared with these explorers, Zheng He's voyages took place much earlier and on a much larger scale. On each of the seven voyages to the Western Seas, his fleet consisted of more than 100 ships, with 62 large and medium-sized ships forming the main body. Crews and other personnel added up to more than 20,000. Columbus' fleet had only three ships and an 88-member crew. Obviously, Zheng He's fleets were unparalleled during his time in terms of size, navigation technology, organization and amenities, in order to be capable of making those successful long trips.

Zheng He's ships were also constructed with advanced technology and craft. A large-size ship in the fleet was 150 meters long, 60 meters wide and 12 meters deep. It had a cargo capacity of about 1,000 tons, with four levels to house more than 1,000 crew and passengers. The foredeck had an area of 9,000 square meters, equal to the size of half a football field. The ship had nine masts with 12 sails. Its iron rudder needed more than 200 people to lift. The large ships of Zheng He's fleet would still look extraordinary even today.

Spreading Peace

When Emperor Yongle sent Zheng He on the missions to the Western Seas, he expected to show off the prosperity of the Ming Empire as well as to put his ideals into practice, of making friends with and spreading peace to other countries near and far. Zheng He's huge fleet was indeed proof of the strength

Blue-and-white plate from the Xuande reign (1426-1435) of the Ming Dynasty

of China at the time. At the same time, the navigator was also fulfilling the emperor's wishes of developing China's international relations.

Zheng He's family chronicles, which came to light in the 1930s, include records of Emperor Yongle's exhortations before his departure: "Follow the ways of Heaven and the world, do not bully small or weak countries, and spread the blessing of peace." On all his voyages Zheng He strictly followed the emperor's instructions.

Although Zheng He brought a large armed force along on all seven long journeys, only on three occasions during those 28 years did he deploy troops. The first time was to wipe out pirates in the Palembang area (southeast of present-day Sumatra), to restore order and transport routes. The second and third times he used force was in self-defense: against an attack by a king of Ceylon (now Sri Lanka), and against a gang of rioters from the Sumatra area. None of these acts constituted a violation of the principle of peace laid down by Emperor Yongle.

Of the many places that Zheng He's fleets reached, they never occupied an inch of anybody's territory, nor took away the slightest bit of anybody's property, nor left a single soldier on anybody's land. Instead, they always presented all sorts of gifts to local kings and their families, chieftains at different levels, and to Buddhist temples. The gifts ranged from cash, silk, porcelain and clothing,

Blue-and-white plate from the Hongwu reign (1368-1398) of the Ming Dynasty

Celadon vase from Yaozhou Kiln of the Song Dynasty

to utensils made of iron, copper, silver and gold. Zheng He even brought bricks, tiles and glazed tiles for locals to build temples in some parts of Southeast Asia. Following principles of fair trade, Zheng He's crew bartered porcelain, silk, tea, and metal utensils with local governments and ordinary citizens for jewelry, spices, medicine, and rare animals. They also introduced to the countries they visited items such as: the Chinese calendar, Chinese medical sciences, and technologies in farming, manufacturing, navigation and shipbuilding.

On every one of his missions, Zheng He would bring envoys from other lands back to China. For example, in the ninth lunar month of 1422 (20th year of Emperor Yongle's reign), more than 1,200 envoys from 16 states in Southern Africa came to visit China with Zheng He's fleet. There were also several kings who traveled on Zheng He's ship back to China. Three of them – from Sulu (now Sulu Archipelago of the Philippines), Borneo (today's Kalimantan Island) and Gran Molucas (now Mindanao Island of the Philippines) – stayed in China until they died due to illness. When the king of Borneo died in 1408, Emperor Yongle called a recess of the court for three days of mourning.

People in some Asian countries still retain fond memories of Zheng He's visits. One can find many commemorative buildings in these countries, such as the temple named after Zheng

He in the Indonesian port city of Semarang. In the Malacca Straits area there can be found a well said to have been dug by Zheng He. In 2004, in celebration of the 30th anniversary of the establishment of diplomatic ties between Malaysia and China, the Royal Opera House in Kuala Lumpur staged a large bilingual song-and-dance drama in Chinese and Malay. Based on *Sejarah Melayu*, or *The Malay Annals*, the drama presented the story of Princess Hanbaoli, daughter of Emperor Yongle, who was escorted by Zheng He and a 500-member retinue to her wedding with Sultan Mansur Shah of Malacca. This is one of the many fine stories about the travels of Zheng He.

10. The Great Wall

No discussion about Chinese culture is complete without mention of the Great Wall. Through more than 2,000 years from the seventh century BC to the 16th century AD, 19 dynasties built parts of the Great Wall, adding up to over 100,000 kilometers. Three major renovations of the Great Wall took place in the Qin (221-206 BC), Han (206 BC-AD 220), and Ming (1368-1644) dynasties. The Great Wall of today is mainly the legacy of the Ming-dynasty renovations. It meanders for 6,700 kilometers from Jiayu Pass in the western desert to Shanhai Pass on the eastern seashore. With many gaps along the Wall, the 600-kilometer-long section in the northern outskirts of Beijing is the best preserved.

Aspiration for Peace

The Great Wall is unparalleled in the world in its scale and span of construction, as well as for the great quantities of labor and the degree of difficulty involved. During the reign of the First Emperor of Qin (r. 246-210 BC), one out of every 20 people took part in the project. Why did the Chinese build the Great Wall? There must be a reason for this ancient nation to build such a wall over a time span of more than 2,000 years.

The earliest parts of the Great Wall were built amid incessant wars. Suffering from the devastating damage of wars, people realized that building a wall to protect lives was better than burying the dead in trenches. Building walls was extremely hard labor, sometimes even at the cost of life itself. Compared with bloody wars, however, people would rather choose the former. Thus the Great Wall was built with the basic goal of safeguarding peace. It represented people's longing for a peaceful life.

The Great Wall played a significant role in history. It certainly served the purposes of military defense in the age of cold steel, especially in preventing northern peoples on horseback from attacking people in the south who were

An observation and defense tower on the Great Wall

mostly engaged in farming. It provided the cultivators with a sense of security as well as actual protection, so they could till their lands and harvest their crops in peace.

Separation and Integration

The geographic structure and climatic patterns of China has led to the development of two distinct cultures from ancient times. The south, with arable land and a warm climate, was suited for agriculture. The north, with pastoral land and a cold climate, was suited for animal husbandry. The south had a relatively developed agricultural civilization, while the north was in a relatively less developed state. Stability was important for an agricultural population. The northern peoples, on the other hand, were highly mobile due to the nature of pastoral life. The limited and unstable output of animal husbandry made it necessary for the northern peoples to depend on the agricultural goods of the southern peoples. Historically, invasions of the south by nomadic peoples of the north were often more out of necessity than the desire for expansion.

From the Qin of more than 2,000 years ago to the later dynasties, the northern peoples who often invaded the south included the Xianyun, the Hun, the Tujue, the Huihe, the Qidan, the Nüzhen, and the Mongolian. Southern troops were often at a disadvantage in the face of the mobile northern cavalry. Under such circumstances, the Great Wall provided an effective, though not perfect, defense line.

In this way, the Great Wall separated the peoples of the south and the north, while posing a barrier to communication. However, it did serve to minimize conflicts between the two, making it possible for each to develop on their own. The Wall protected the agricultural economy and advanced the mode of production in the south. At the same time, it forced the northern peoples to give up plundering the south and to develop their own civilization. This laid the foundation for later exchange and communication between the southern and northern cultures.

Chinese history would have been another story without the Great Wall. Dr. Sun Yat-sen (1866-1925), who led the Revolution of 1911 that overthrew the Qing Dynasty (1616-1911), said, "Seen from today, if it had not been for the protection of the Great Wall, Chinese civilization would have been interrupted by the northern peoples in the late Qin or early Han dynasties, long before the Song (960-1279) and Ming dynasties. In that case, there would not have been the prosperity of the Han and Tang (618-907) dynasties, or the integration of southern and northern peoples."

In time, economic zones came into being along the Great Wall, especially at its several dozen passes, where people from both sides carried out economic and

Part of the Mutianyu
section of the Great Wall,
in the northern suburbs
of Beijing

cultural exchanges. For a long time in history, the agricultural economy in the south and the pastoral economy in the north complemented and depended on each other through such exchanges. In this way, the Great Wall played a role in bringing in a new economic structure to the benefit of both sides.

Spirit of the Great Wall

The hardships involved in building the Great Wall are beyond imagination. Numerous people had to leave their homes and families to go north, where they toiled for years. Many lost their lives on the worksites, over a period of more than 2,000 years. A Chinese idiom vividly expresses the Great Wall as the achievement of many, "Efforts joined by many can build the Great Wall."

Of the many legends about the Great Wall, the story of Lady Mengjiang is the most moving. Lady Mengjiang lived during the reign of the First Emperor of Qin. After her husband was recruited to build the Great Wall, she missed him so much that she traveled many miles to see him. When she finally arrived at the construction site, a fellow countryman told her that her husband had died and was buried under the Wall. A heartbroken Lady Mengjiang cried for three days and nights until, legend has it, the Great Wall collapsed one section after another.

People paid an enormous price for the building of the Great Wall. The legend of Lady Mengjiang represents the sufferings of the people. It also expressed their hatred for the tyrannical First Emperor of Qin. It was not a condemnation of the Great Wall itself, because the people had no reason to resent this defensive work that protected them. The builders of the Wall were no "cowards who chose to close themselves up," as some people so claim, but heroes with a unanimous will and unparalleled strength.

Over the centuries, the Great Wall has become a symbol of consolidation and strength for the Chinese people. It symbolizes that great achievement can be made with a common will and concerted effort. For example, the national anthem, composed during the War of Resistance Against Japanese Aggression

Part of the Simatai section of the Great Wall, in the northern suburbs of Beijing

(1937-1945), called on the people to "build our new Great Wall with our flesh and blood."

Wonder of the Great Wall

The wonder of the Great Wall lies in its magnificent and varied structure. As a defense work, the Great Wall is by no means a monotonous long stretch of wall. Instead, it consists of different parts with different defensive purposes. These include blockhouses, garrison towns and passes built at strategic points, as well as beacon towers along the wall.

The Simatai section built near Beijing in the Ming Dynasty best represents the undulating and rhythmic flow of the Great Wall. As a popular saying has it, Simatai epitomizes the wonder of the Great Wall for being the most precipitous part of it.

Winding along a steep ridge of a range of mountains, the Simatai section rises to the crests of mountains at some points and falls into deep valleys at others. The most breathtaking parts of the Simatai section are called Cloud Ladder and Heavenly Bridge. The Cloud Ladder is much narrower than the normal width of the Wall (three-to-five meters on average), the narrowest part being only half a meter wide. With perilous cliffs on either side, it indeed resembles a ladder along which one can climb up into the clouds. Up at the top of the Cloud Ladder, one comes to the Heavenly Bridge, the 100-meter-long narrow belt of wall on the mountain ridge, with deep valleys on either side.

A precipitous part of the Simatai section of the Great Wall

The highest point of the Simatai section is Wangjing (Overlooking the Capital) Tower, at an altitude of 986 meters. From here, one can capture a panoramic overview of the Great Wall stretching and winding into the east and west. One can also look into the far distance to the south, for an indistinct view of the capital Beijing. Hence, the name of the tower. This is one of the best places to appreciate the magnificence and near-surreal beauty of the Great Wall.

11. The Forbidden City: Glorious and Awe-inspiring

The Forbidden City, also known as the Palace Museum, is where 24 emperors of the Ming (1368-1644) and Qing (1616-1911) dynasties ruled China from the 15th century to the early 20th century. It is the most splendid palace complex in Beijing and one of the best preserved of its kind in the world. Its awe-inspiring architecture and huge variety of collections stand as living evidence to the rich historical essence of this country.

Concealed Contours of a Dragon

When Emperor Yongle (r. 1403-1424) decided to make Beijing his capital, he also decided to follow the design of the central axis of Dadu – the name for Beijing when it served as the capital of the Yuan Dynasty (1206-1368). Of course, the Ming emperor had also commissioned a large-scale redesign of the overall structure of his new capital. Construction of the magnificent imperial city took nearly 1 million people many decades to complete.

Night view of the Front Gate on Tiananmen Square

The Ming capital was built along an eight-kilometer-long axis running south to north. Buildings and landscapes were laid out on either side of the axis. The overall design featured symmetry between left and right, along the axis, giving the city a unique sublime order.

The axis starts from the Gate of Eternal Stability in the south. On the east side of the axis stands the Temple of Heaven and on the west is the Temple for the Divine Cultivator, the two being in approximate symmetry. As sites for offering sacrifices to Heaven and the Divine Cultivator, the two structures truly deserve the status of being the starting points of the city's axis. Originally, a straight boulevard led to the grand Front Gate. A huge stone archway and a large stone bridge used to stand north of the Front Gate, which represented the first rise of the axis south of the city. Further north stood the China Gate, which was demolished in 1959 to make way for Tiananmen Square.

Located to the north of the square is the Gate of Heavenly Peace. During the Ming it was called Gate for Receiving Heavenly Favor. To the east of Tiananmen is the Imperial Family Shrine (where the emperor would pay homage to his ancestors), and to its west, the Imperial State Shrine (honoring the gods of land and grain). Today, the former is known as the Working People's Cultural Palace, and the latter has become Sun Yat-sen Park. Placing the two temples on an equal footing has a great deal to do with China's history as an agrarian society. Through the Gate of Uprightness and then the Meridian Gate, the central axis passes into the Forbidden City, and extends all the way to its northern gate, Gate of Divine Might. To the north of the Gate of Divine Might is Prospect Hill, which provides a backdrop for the Forbidden City. The central peak of the hill, graced by a pavilion, is directly above the central axis. Further north

A bird's-eye-view of the Forbidden City

Golden Water Bridges to the north of the Tiananmen Rostrum

to Prospect Hill is the Gate of Earthly Peace. From there a straight boulevard leads to the Drum Tower and the Bell Tower, which mark the northern end of the central axis of ancient Beijing.

The Forbidden City, covering an area of 720,000 square meters, consists of the Outer Court (southern part) and the Inner Court (northern part). The Outer Court is where the emperor ran state affairs, and the Inner Court is where the imperial family lived. The main structures of the Outer Court are the Hall of Supreme Harmony, the Hall of Central Harmony and the Hall for Preserving Harmony. The Hall of Supreme Harmony is located in the very center of the Forbidden City. To the east of the three main halls is the Hall of Literary Glory and to their west stands the Hall of Military Eminence, for civil and military administration respectively. The main structures of the Inner Court are the Hall of Heavenly Purity, the Hall of Union and Peace, and the Hall of Earthly Tranquility. On either side of these halls are the Eastern Six Palaces and the Western Six

Palaces, living quarters for the imperial concubines. There are over 8,000 halls and rooms in the Forbidden City, all laid out in a precise manner along the central axis or to its sides.

The central axis that runs from the south to the north of Beijing resembles the undulating contours of a dragon. The buildings along the central line and on either side of it vary in design and rhythm. Of the eight-kilometer-long axis, the section from the Gate of Eternal Stability to the Front Gate represents its gentle beginnings, while the section from the Front Gate through the Forbidden City to Prospect Hill is the peak, and the section from Prospect Hill to the Drum and Bell Towers concludes it. Appreciating Old Beijing is thus like appreciating the three stages of a musical movement.

The Colors of the Forbidden City

No one can visit the Forbidden City without marveling at its unique application of color.

Yellow and vermilion are the thematic colors of the Forbidden City. Yellow was symbolic of imperial power in ancient China, and red has always been symbolic of happiness. Being bright colors, they give a sense of warmth and passion.

All of the nearly 1,000 individual buildings in the Forbidden City have roofs covered with golden glazed tiles and vermilion walls. The red color of the numerous pillars supporting the buildings also has a strong visual impact. On a clear day, the panorama presented by glistening golden tiles on top of red buildings under a blue sky resembles a dreamland among the green trees surrounding the Forbidden City.

Besides yellow and red, other colors are used to produce a balanced effect. For example, the beams under the eaves are usually painted with pictures in cool colors such as blue and white. Red pillars, doors and windows usually stand on a white stone floor. The gold and red buildings, against the huge white marble terraces on which they stand, form a striking contrast in color. Take the Hall of Supreme Harmony, for example. When observed from its east side, the hall resembles a colorful heavenly palace floating in a kingdom of white clouds – the enormous three-tiered marble terrace on which it stands.

While bright yellow and red colors give prominence to imperial power, blue, white and similar cool colors add an element of grace to the buildings. For example, the spacious courtyard between the Gate of Uprightness (to the south) and the Gate of Supreme Harmony (to the north) is entirely paved with gray bricks. Five marble bridges span the Inner Golden River just inside the Gate of Uprightness. Against this gray background rises the Gate of Supreme Harmony in radiant gold and red, a vision of extreme magnificence.

No visitor to the Forbidden City can help but be stricken by the awe-inspiring sights of this historic wonder in the center of Beijing.

Night view of one of the two watchtowers of the Forbidden City, at its northeast and northwest corners.

Art and Aesthetics

The Chinese have created many unique forms of art – gorgeous bronzeware, elegant gardens, natural ink-and-wash paintings, pure porcelain, enduring Tang poetry, free-flowing calligraphy, timeless statues of the Buddha, and colorful Peking opera. These art forms reveal the inner world of the Chinese people and represent their unique sense of aesthetics. The Chinese regard art as a way to enhance the quality of life and to soothe the mind. It is an extension of the Chinese philosophy on life.

12. *Music: Govern the Country, Nourish the Mind*

The tradition of Chinese music dates back to remote antiquity. Governing the country and nourishing the mind through music are two of the main functions of this tradition.

Governance Through Music

According to ancient Chinese culture, rituals provided the norms of conduct for people. The goal was to maintain social order. Music was for the mind's cultivation and expression. Its purpose was to enhance people's outlook on life and imbue them with energy and creativity, such that they could enjoy a more harmonious and happier spiritual life. Individual contentment would then lead to social harmony, as well as to a more harmonious relationship between people and nature. The highest level of ancient Chinese music was to represent spiritual harmony with nature.

Marquis Yi chime bells (detail)

The prominent stature of music in ancient China explains the emergence of sophisticated instruments from early times. Chime bells were one example. First used in the Shang Dynasty (1600-1046 BC), they became quite popular during the Western Zhou Dynasty (1046-771 BC). In 1978, a fine set of chime bells was unearthed in Hubei Province, from the tomb of Marquis Yi, a local lord in a small state called Zeng during the Warring States Period (475-221 BC).

The Marquis Yi chime bells consist of 65 bells arranged in three rows. The first row includes 19 *niu* bells, and the second and third rows include 45 *yong* bells. The bells in each row differ from one another in shape and size, emanating different tones. In addition, there is a separate and much larger bell used to adjust pitch. Like the bells, the frame is made of bronze, weighing as much as five tons or more. The total weight of the bells is more than 440 kilograms.

While the bells bear inscriptions totaling more than 2,800 Chinese characters relating to music and the making of the instrument, the frame is carved with exquisite patterns in relief and fretwork. Instruments of such a scale and such fine craftsmanship were quite rare in the world at the time.

Five musicians were needed to play the instrument. Each bell produces two tones when struck at the respective sound points as marked. The entire set of chime bells is able to produce all the tones of a modern piano.

The grandeur and precision of the Marquis Yi chime bells epitomize ancient Chinese society's emphasis on music as a means to promote personal cultivation and social harmony. Xunzi (c. 325-235 BC), a great Confucian thinker of the Warring States Period, gave music the same stature as rituals, stating, "Musical education enables people to purify their minds. Rituals are established to temper people's conduct. With music and rituals, people are imbued with clearer, more intelligent and peaceful minds. They also improve their ways and manners. Thus the country enjoys peace, with beauty and compassion complementing each other."

"Music brings harmony" is an important concept that has influenced Chinese culture

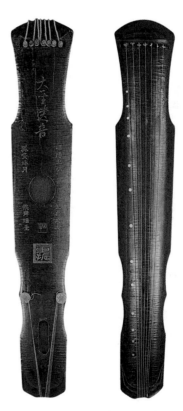

Chinese zither (front and back), said to have been handed down from the Tang Dynasty

for several thousand years. It stresses harmony as the culture's core value. The tradition guiding rituals and music is that of a harmonious world order.

Consoling the Mind with Music

One cannot discuss Chinese music without mentioning a seven-stringed musical instrument, the Chinese zither, which represented the zenith of cultivated learning in ancient times, followed by go, calligraphy and painting. As the most ancient instrument in China, the zither has long been a favorite of the literati. While music in general was meant to govern the country by promoting harmony, the Chinese zither was more of an individual instrument for solace and personal appreciation.

Ancient Chinese literati considered the zither a prerequisite for their cultivation. Its beautiful melodies helped to maintain peace and balance of the mind.

Ambiance was an important aspect in playing the Chinese zither. Zong Bing (375-443), a painter and musician of the late Eastern Jin Dynasty (317-420) and early

Playing the Chinese Zither under Pine Trees, *by Zhu Derun (1294-1365), Yuan Dynasty. The painting evokes a harmonious outlook, as aspired to by Chinese literati, in which the musician is at one with nature.*

Southern Dynasties (420-589), enjoyed playing the zither by a stream in the mountains. As he plucked the strings gently, he would gradually forget where he was. The sounds of the zither mixed with the echoes from the mountains, until the musician found himself at one with nature.

Playing the Chinese zither in snow was also a favorite pastime for ancient artists, who regarded the instrument as the purest of its kind in the world. What could be more fitting than playing it midst white snow? Wu Wei (1409-1508), a famed painter of the Ming Dynasty (1368-1644), described the following scene in the masterpiece *Looking for Plum Blossoms in Snow*. A man with a walking stick is crossing a snow-covered bridge. A page follows him, holding a zither in his arms. Melting snow flows under the bridge, revealing the rugged rocks of the riverbed. This painting represented a dreamland for ancient Chinese artists and scholars.

A moonlit night was also considered ideal for playing the zither. Wang Wei (c. 701-761), a highly accomplished poet of the Tang Dynasty (618-907), liked playing the zither in a bamboo forest on moonlit nights. His poem "In a Bamboo Forest" has these lines: *"Sitting alone in a deep bamboo forest, / I play my zither and whistle along. / No one else around, / I have the moon for company."*

The Chinese zither tends to create a tranquil air. The composition *Wild Geese Landing on the Shallow Shore* is such an example. With a relaxed rhythm, the first part of the piece depicts a calm Yangtze River under a clear autumn sky. The second part progresses into livelier rhythms to imitate the chirping of many birds. The third part presents a thematic scene of wild geese leisurely landing on the shallow shores of the Yangtze, as a gentle breeze makes the water ripple. To Chinese musicians and music lovers, the contentment of the wild geese represents the human heart.

The zither was also instrumental in communication between ancient scholars and artists. The famous zither composition, *Three Stanzas of Plum Blossoms*, was based on an Eastern Jin Dynasty (317-420) story of the poet

Wang Ziyou (c. 338-386) and the flute player Huan Yi (?-383). One day the poet was taking a boat trip when he overheard someone on the riverbank say Huan Yi was passing by. Although the two had never met before, they admired each other as poet and flute player. Despite his lower rank of office, Ziyou sent a family member to request Huan Yi to play the flute. Without hesitation, Huan Yi dismounted from his carriage and played *Three Stanzas of Plum Blossoms*, while Ziyou listened from his boat. After finishing, Huan Yi mounted his carriage and drove on. Ziyou, too, continued with his boat journey. The two of them exchanged not a single word, yet both were content with the communication of their hearts through the music. The flute's three stanzas were later converted into a composition for the Chinese zither, which has become one of the best-known musical works – as an expression of otherworldly feelings through its eulogy of the plum flowers' purity, fragrance and resistance to the cold.

13. Spiritual Essence in Bronzeware

The Bronze Age refers to the period when bronze tools and weapons were commonly used. The Bronze Age in China lasted more than 1,500 years, from the Xia (2070-1600 BC) through the Shang (1600-1046 BC) and Western Zhou (1046-771 BC) dynasties, to the Spring and Autumn Period (770-476 BC). Large numbers of unearthed artifacts indicate a high level of ancient bronze civilization in the country. They feature rich political and religious themes, and are of high artistic value.

Great Ding for Yu

The *ding* was originally a cauldron for cooking, with three legs and two ears as handles. It later evolved into a ritual object. A representative example is the *Great* Ding *for Yu*, cast about 3,000 years ago during the reign of King Kang (1020-994 BC) of the Western Zhou Dynasty. Now preserved in the Museum of Chinese History, the huge *ding*, more than a meter tall, is characteristic of the solemnity of the ritual objects of that time.

During the Shang and Zhou dynasties, those in power were keen to cast large-size bronzeware as state ritual objects or symbols of their power. The king of a state would bestow bronzeware on his officials to show his authority, while the latter would receive such articles as an honor. The *Great* Ding *for Yu* illustrates this power relationship. Its interior is inscribed with 291 characters, unusually numerous for similar bronze objects of the period. They were instructions by King Kang to General Yu, warning him against drinking. The general was about to launch an expedition, and the king was reminding him of the fall of the Shang Dynasty, which had been replaced by Western Zhou.

Great *Ding* for Yu, one of the representative works of China's Bronze Age

The body of the *Great* Ding *for Yu* and its three legs bear images of a *taotie*, a legendary animal notorious for its greed for food. The *tiaotie* has a head with a huge mouth. It does not have a body. It is not clear why such a strange, greedy beast was popularly used to decorate bronze ritual objects. One possible reason was probably to use its malevolent image to ward off evil.

Lotus and Crane Kettles

A pair of square bronze kettles from the late Spring and Autumn Period are two outstanding artifacts from China's Bronze Age. Their name comes from the ornamental themes on the kettles. Compared with the solid and solemn style of bronzeware in the Western Zhou Dynasty, the square kettles are light in stature and graceful in style. The exquisite carvings on the kettles feature smooth lines and elaborate designs without looking too crowded.

The square kettles are not exactly square, as the four sides of each are not exactly of the same width. The neck is a little narrower than the body, which bulges towards the bottom. Two dragon-like animals are attached to two facing sides, which seem to serve as handles. A legendary beast clings onto each of the four lower corners. Two strange beasts hold up the kettle from underneath the bottom rim. The lid is decorated with a ring of lotus petals, arranged in two layers resembling a lotus in full bloom. At the center of the lotus flower is perched a crane, stretching its neck and flapping its wings.

The heavy body of the kettle and the light crane on the lid set off each other, as do the exotic patterns on the surface of the kettle and the elegant posture of the crane.

Aside from the flying crane and the two beasts on the bottom, with their tails coiling upwards, the smaller flying dragons on the neck and the swimming dragons on the lower part of the kettle all imbue the heavy bronze object with a sense of motion. In particular, the fully open lotus petals resemble a floating cloud, on which the crane flies.

Lotus and Crane Square Kettle, *with the lid's flying crane evoking a sense of motion*

Galloping Horse Overtaking a Flying Swallow

Cast during the Eastern Han Dynasty (25-220), *Galloping Horse Overtaking a Flying Swallow* stands out as an immortal work of sculpture in the history of Chinese art.

The horse was an important subject in ancient Chinese sculpture. *Galloping Horse Overtaking a Flying Swallow* differs from the other sculptures of horses in that it represents motion, rather than the horse itself.

When a horse gallops full speed, it looks as if it were flying in the air. So the ancient Chinese thought of a fast horse as a "heavenly steed soaring in the skies." Usually, the sculpture of a swift horse had to be set atop a floating cloud.

Galloping Horse Overtaking a Flying Swallow, *Eastern Han Dynasty,*
representing the artistic imagination of a heavenly horse flying through the skies

Galloping Horse Overtaking a Flying Swallow, however, has one of its hind hoofs set on a swallow in flight, while the other legs are airborne. The horse holds its head high, with its eyes staring, its nostrils flaring and its ears up. Part of the mane is standing erect, while the tail thrown up in the air. Its body features strong, smooth muscles, and its belly is contracted as it runs. As the galloping horse overtakes the tiny swallow, the latter turns back to look at it in surprise.

One would normally imagine that a swallow flies faster than a galloping horse. Now that the horse has overtaken the swallow, it inspires the viewer to imagine how fast the horse is running. Li Bai (701-762), one of the best-known poets of the Tang Dynasty (618-907), wrote the poem "Song of the Heavenly Horse". Two of the lines can be borrowed to describe this sculpture: *"Looking back at the black swallow, / (The horse) laughs at its slowness."*

14. A Silent Army

Renowned as one of the "Eight Wonders of the World," the Terracotta Army of the First Emperor of Qin (r. 246-210 BC) is not only a great legacy of his military might, but also a superb paradigm of ancient Chinese sculpture.

Discovery of the Terracotta Army

In the spring of 1974, when villagers were digging a well near Xianyang, Shaanxi Province, they came across unusual pottery fragments. Some resembled human figures, while others looked like animals. Word of the chance findings alerted archeologists, who soon uncovered on the site a huge army of terracotta warriors and horses, which had been interred with the remains of the First Emperor more than 2,000 years ago.

Altogether, four pits housing thousands of terracotta warriors have been unearthed, numbered according to the time sequence of their discovery. Pit No. 1, with an area of more than 14,000 square meters, is the largest. It is home to an entire battle formation of life-size soldiers and horses. The front echelon consists of 210 soldiers standing in three rows, with the commander in the front. About 6,000 soldiers make up the main body of the formation. They stand in 38

A crouching warrior, just unearthed from Pit. No. 2, his martial bearing untarnished by the soil still on his face

columns, some as long as 180 meters. All of them sport suits of armor and hold bronze weapons. On either side of the central echelon is a row of 180 soldiers, as flanks of the formation. At the back, more than 100 warriors stand, probably part of the rear guard. Among the formation are 32 terracotta horses, with four drawing a wooden war chariot.

As the most imposing of all the battle formations discovered so far, Pit No. 1 is most likely a replica of the actual troops during the First Emperor's lifetime.

Pits No. 2 and 3 were discovered in the summer of 1976.

Pits No. 2 has four battle formations, including more than 1,300 soldiers and horses, over 80 war chariots, and tens of thousands of bronze weapons. In the eastern section of the pit is a group of archers. At the front are 60 archers standing upright, followed by eight columns totaling 160 archers squatting on one leg and kneeling on the other. To their right is a formation of 64 war chariots arranged in eight rows. Each chariot is drawn by four life-size horses. Behind every chariot stand three soldiers: the one in the middle holds the reins, while the two on the sides are holding long-staffed weapons.

In the middle of Pit No. 2 is another chariot formation, consisting of 19 chariots, 264 infantry men and eight horsemen. They are divided into three rows. At the front of each horse stands a soldier, with one hand holding the reins and the other in the pose of pulling a bow. Behind each chariot are three charioteers, followed by a number of foot soldiers. To the left of the chariots is a formation of 108 horsemen and 180 saddled horses in 11 rows.

Pit No. 3 is located to the west of Pit No. 1. In a 凹 shape, it is the smallest of all the pits, with only 68 warriors inside. A war chariot was placed at the front of the entrance. The formation resembles the headquarters of the left, central and right divisions of the entire army, but it was probably not completed.

Pit No. 4 was discovered much later, covering an area of about 5,000 square meters. Located between Pits No. 2 and 3, it appears to have been planned to house the central division, but was filled up without any warriors or horses.

Head of a standing archer, in Pit. No. 2, his eyes observing the enemy in the distance

Vivid Sculpture

The terracotta warriors and horses caused a sensation upon their discovery, not only because of the impressive size of the army, but also due to the masterful craftsmanship of the sculptures.

All the soldiers and horses are life-size, the former about 1.85 meters tall and the latter 1.6 meters in height. The original figures were colorfully painted, but most of the color was lost after long years of burial. The sculptures are realistic representations of real-life models, without any exaggeration or distortion. All the warriors are distinctive in terms of hairstyle, eyes, eyebrows, nose, lips, ears and beards, showing their individual age, position and personality. Both soldiers and horses look vivid and exude a sense of dynamic motion.

For example, the half-squatting, half-kneeling archers in Pit No. 2 each have their hair tied in a knot and wear suits of armor over their war robes. They genuflect on one leg while squatting on the other, their bodies leaning forward and their hands pulling bows. Although no bows or arrows survived the long years underground, the archers' posture clearly shows the tension of the process of shooting. The standing archers feature strong bodies and highly alert expressions, with eyebrows lowered, nostrils slightly flaring and ears alert. Listening attentively, they seem ready to strike at the first signal of battle. Even the suits of armor have different creases to show the movements of the different soldiers. A range of use of body strength in the half-squatting and half-kneeling archers is also discernible. Such vivid representation of detail helps to create the illusion that the warriors are actually alive.

There are more than 600 terracotta horses in the three pits. These, too, closely resemble real horses. Some are pulling chariots, while others are cavalry steeds. Take one of the cavalry horses in Pit No. 2 for example. It is standing firmly

A crouching archer, in Pit. No. 2, a fine example of sculptural art of the time

One of several restored chariots drawn by four horses,
from Pit. No. 2, a superb bronze artwork

behind a cavalry soldier. It seems to be raising its front legs while keeping its hind legs steady on the ground. The horse holds its head high, with its mane standing erect. Its tail, while remaining still, is turned a little upwards. The head features clear-chiseled lines, looking sturdy and neat. With flaring nostrils, a gently closed mouth and wide-open eyes, the horse appears highly vigilant and dynamic.

The Terracotta Army of the First Emperor of Qin has enabled people of today to attain a new understanding of the great sculptural arts of over 2,000 years ago, through realistic and vivid representations of an unprecedented number of warriors, horses and chariots.

15. The Eternal Smile of the Buddha

Buddhism found its way to China around the first century and has since exerted a significant, far-reaching influence on Chinese culture. It has left an indelible mark on Chinese art, with splendid Buddhist artistic works surviving the vicissitudes of time. Among them, statues of the Buddha constitute an important component, and are found in many places across the country, including the Yungang Grottoes in Shanxi Province, the Mogao Grottoes in Gansu Province, the Longmen Grottoes in Henan Province, the Dazu Stone Sculptures in Chongqing Municipality, as well as in numerous temples. The Buddha statues, in a sense, record the development of Chinese civilization, displaying the achievements of sculptural arts and expressing the aspirations of the people.

Beautiful Guanyin in the Mogao Grottoes

The Mogao Grottoes in Dunhuang are considered the foremost representative of grotto arts. Dunhuang, once a town of strategic importance on the Silk Road, is located east of present-day Lanzhou, the capital city of Gansu Province in northwestern China. Over a span of nearly 1,000 years from the fourth century to the 14th century, a great number of people came here to build grottoes on the precipitous cliffs of Mingsha Mountain, ultimately turning this place into an artistic treasure-house combining architecture, painted sculptures and murals. As the statues and paintings mostly depict the Buddha, people also call this place "The Cave of One Thousand Buddha Statues."

In Grotto 45 in Dunhuang, a Buddha statue: grace with a loving heart

Guanyin or the Goddess of Mercy, known also as the Bodhisattva, is a sage second only to Sakyamuni, the founder of Buddhism. She is popular among the people for her benevolence and readiness to ease those in distress. It is believed that anyone facing a disaster or danger will be saved as long as they chant her name. The Chinese people have been worshipping Guanyin for more than 1,000 years, through ceremonies still existing today in some areas. A performance named "Guanyin with 1,000 Hands," first put onstage by the China Dance Troupe of Disabled Persons several years ago, has been hailed by audiences the world over, and is in itself an expression of people's devotion to the Goddess of Mercy.

The Mogao Grottoes are an impressive reflection of the

rituals of worshipping Guanyin. There are many statues of the goddess, such as Guanyin with 1,000 hands and 1,000 eyes, and Guanyin with 11 faces. The Goddess of Mercy was originally a male Buddha in Indian Buddhism, but after he was introduced into China he gradually transformed into a woman, becoming the embodiment of all good human qualities, such as gentleness, kindness and tolerance.

In Grotto 45 are two painted statues of Guanyin, completed in the Tang Dynasty (618-907). The two statues are alike in appearance, with a chignon on the head, a celestial robe covering half the upper body, crescent eyebrows, gentle eyes faintly smiling, and a bright and benevolent expression. Both wear necklaces, with their arms plump and their robes long with a lotus design showing underneath. They stand in an elegant S-shape posture, one foot on the ground, the other slightly off the ground, and their bodies gracefully tilting to one side.

Both painted statues have a benign countenance, lovable eyes and elegant bearing. They look so vivid that they resemble pretty damsels of the earthly world rather than a goddess. These sculptures demonstrate people's devotion toward the benevolent Guanyin and eulogize maternal love and feminine beauty.

Smiling Buddha in the Maijishan Grottoes

As one of the four famous grottoes in China, the Maijishan (Haystack Mountain) Grottoes are appreciated for the quality and quantity of the clay sculptures enshrined there. Located southeast of Tianshui City in Gansu Province, Maijishan got its name from its haystack-like shape.

The sculptures in the Maijishan Grottoes evoke a strong secular flavor alongside the obvious influence of Indian sculpture. The statues, though representing the Buddha and his disciples, are wrought with as many human features as possible. The countenance of the statues expresses calm compassion, rather than the more usual far and distant facial expression. The majority of the statues nod and smile in a natural manner, and the contours of their robes are smooth as if flying.

The group of sculptures in Grotto 44 built during the Western Wei Dynasty (535-556) is exemplary of the Buddha statues in the Maijishan Grottoes. The main Buddha statue, sitting in the center of the group of sculptures, is 160 centimeters tall with a woman's figure, who wears his hair in a chignon with a whirlpool pattern, his hairline executed in a cloud shape. An ornamental knot decorates his chest, and a kasaya wraps his shoulders and cascades down, with

In Grotto 44 in Maijishan, a Buddha statue: facing the despondent secular world with a smile

the draping curves of the robe smoothly, clearly and beautifully outlined. Traces of color can be seen on his clothing and hairline. He has long and thin eyebrows, a slightly inclined head, smiling mysteriously and kindly. One can only imagine how beautiful the statue must have been when it made its debut in this world!

According to the Buddhist sutras, when Sakyamuni gave a sermon, he always smiled. This statue has not only a smile on his face but a smile seeming to spread all over his body. The smiling countenance and the gentle contours of his body effectively display the Buddha's magnanimity, composure and elegance.

When this collection of statues in Grotto 44 was created, China was experiencing one of the most traumatic periods in its history, with endless wars claiming the lives of countless people, and the survivors plunged into an abyss of suffering. These statues face the despondent secular world with a smile and magnanimity, thus giving people faith in life.

Buddha of Brightness in the Longmen Grottoes

The Longmen Grottoes, located in the southern suburbs of Luoyang, Henan Province, have a history of more than 1,500 years.

In the Tang Dynasty, Empress Wu (r. 690-704), sponsored the construction of the largest of the Longmen Grottoes – the Temple of Ancestral Worship. Inside the temple is a huge statue of Sambhoga-kaya Buddha, or the Buddha of Brightness, which took three years to finish. On the day of its completion, Empress Wu led her ministers to the consecration ceremony, one of the most important cultural events of the Tang Dynasty.

The statue of the Buddha of Brightness sits at an imposing height of more than 17 meters. It is the largest of all the statues found in the Longmen Grottoes. Buddhist scriptures describe the Buddha of Brightness as the ideal reincarnation of Sakyamuni. With his power of eternal brightness, he is able to eradicate darkness in the human world and bestow enlightenment on the common people.

Buddha of Brightness
in Longmen Grottoes,
Luoyang, Henan
Province

Sitting peacefully and gracefully at the center of the Temple of Ancestral
Worship, the Buddha of Brightness wears a serene expression, facing the world
with dignified composure. Smiling faintly with the corners of his mouth slightly
upturned, he tilts his head a bit forward, commanding a wide view of what is
below him. The aura of calm around him has a soothing effect for countless
troubled souls.

Compassionate Buddha of Qingzhou

In October 1996, a cave was accidentally discovered at a construction site in
Qingzhou of Shandong Province. Archeologists found more than 400 exquisite
Buddha statues from the Northern Qi Dynasty (550-577). This was one of the
most exciting archeological findings of 20th century China. Since 2001, these

statues have been exhibited in Germany, France and the United States, arousing great interest among viewers.

The statues are either sculpted in the round or with their backs in the stone wall. Their postures, standing or sitting, are so vivid and varied that they add touches of liveliness to the solemn ambience of the caves. One particular statue presents an innocent and lovable image of the Buddha with his left foot on a lotus footing and his right foot on his left knee. Although his left arm is missing, the audience may still visualize with their mind's eye that his left hand caresses his right foot.

Another statue in the sitting posture looks light and lithe, and brims with a graceful bearing, his creaseless clothes setting off the contours of his body. He has fine and delicate features and a slim figure. One hand has been damaged, and the other hand is raised before his chest; so he must have been holding his palms together in greeting. Generally speaking, Buddha statues always emphasize natural and calm facial expressions, but the sculptors of the Qingzhou statues placed more emphasis on the meticulous depiction of movement, their most evocative aspect. These statues, while portraying the spirit of Buddhist teachings from a distant land, demonstrate more of an unaffected, ardent local flavor.

From the Northern Qi Dynasty, unearthed in Qingzhou, Shandong Province, a painted Buddha statue: with a mysterious smile and moving luminosity

What is unforgettable about the Qingzhou statues is, more than anything else, their smiles. Smiling Buddha statues are common, but the Qingzhou statues have their own distinctive characteristics. The difference lies in the smiles of the Qingzhou statues not being the usual mysterious smile but rather calm, sweet and reserved. Long, narrow eyes and cherry-like mouths are set off by faintly smiling cheeks. It is a contagious joy rising from their innermost world, spreading from the soul to the body, and on to their postures and even their robes.

The discovery of the Qingzhou Grotto transported smiles from a thousand years ago to today's human world.

16. Flying Strokes of Calligraphy

Today, anyone who knows a little bit about Chinese culture usually knows about Chinese calligraphy. This unique art is related to writing, but speaks of much more than simple, even attractive, penmanship. Actually, although we use "calligraphy" to refer to this art of writing, this English word is unable to cover all its connotations.

The evolution of Chinese calligraphy has benefited from two factors: one is the square-shaped pictographic characters, whose beautiful forms provided preliminary conditions for the art of calligraphy; and the other is the writing brush, an important invention in the history of Chinese culture and the basis for calligraphy to germinate and develop. The writing brush, made from either rabbit, sheep or wolf hair, feels soft, supple, and is elastic and highly ductile. It paved the way for the emergence of the art of calligraphy.

Rhythm of Calligraphy

Calligraphy is the art of lines, or strokes. Lin Huaimin (b. 1947), a famous dancer from China's Taiwan Island and director of the Cloud Gate Dancing Troupe, once choreographed a collective dance named "Running-Cursive Script," which gained him worldwide fame. His inspirations came from Chinese calligraphy, and dancing enlivened the spirit of the art of writing, especially his "Running-Cursive Script No. 2." The dancer onstage becomes no more a dancer but a calligrapher wielding his brush and applying ink to paper, pausing one moment and writing in high spirits the next. His movements are now swift, smooth and elegant, and now slow, gentle and enchanting. Although there is neither script in the setting nor characters on the stage, the audience can easily feel the presence of the intriguing art of calligraphy.

In the Tang Dynasty (618-907), the master calligrapher Zhang Xu (birth and death dates unknown) became absorbed all day long in his world of running-cursive script, copying the master calligraphers from former dynasties, but making little progress. One day, on the streets of Chang'an, the capital city of the dynasty, he saw a crowd of people gathering to enjoy a performance by Lady Gongsun, a famous dancer of the time. She was performing a sword dance, her supple body and flying robe mixing with the movements of the sword up and down, and becoming perfectly integrated into the surroundings. Zhang

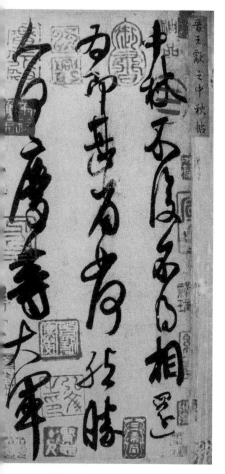

Mid-Autumn, by
Wang Xianzhi
(344-386): a precious
work of Chinese
calligraphy

Xu was enchanted, and it was through this performance that he discovered the genuine beauty of calligraphy and made rapid progress in his profession.

A modern dancer obtained great wisdom from calligraphy, while an ancient calligrapher had been inspired by dance. This definitely indicates some common element that calligraphy and dance share, and this element is none other than their internal vital energy, the soul of calligraphy as well as the soul of dance.

Someone once remarked that enjoying Chinese calligraphy is just like enjoying shadow boxing, in which a boxer moves and turns, making rhythmical, coherent dancing lines in midair.

The "one-stroke character" in Chinese calligraphy refers to such an internal line of energy. A "one-stroke character" actually means a character written with

Temple of Guan Yu, in small regular script by Zhu Yunming
(1460-1527), Ming Dynasty

strokes at one go, rather than implying only one single stroke. The strokes may not look connected on the exterior but are closely related in the interior. Without interior linkage, a character lacks vigor and vitality.

The "one-stroke character" was first advocated by Wang Xianzhi (344-386), son of the most famous calligrapher, Wang Xizhi (303-361) of the Eastern Jin Dynasty (317-420). Wang Xianzhi's *Yatou Wan*, a masterpiece surviving to this day, was thus written at one go, with a rhythmical line of vital energy only intermittently broken. When appreciating such an artistic work, viewers are always deeply impressed and inspired by its inner lines, without even being conscious of it.

Chinese calligraphy is set against the brushwork of the "ink pig." The so-called ink pig refers to calligraphic work in heavy, dense ink, which fails to give play to vigorous brushwork, resulting in fat strokes and cumbersome handwriting resembling a fat pig. This is exactly due to the lack of vigorous lines and internal energy.

Preface to the Lanting Pavilion Collection, *by Wang Xizhi (303-361), Eastern Jin Dynasty: a gem of Chinese calligraphy*

Wang Xizhi and *Preface to the Lanting Pavilion Collection*

In the Hall for Cultivation of Mind of the Palace Museum, there is a Three-treasure Study, which derives its name for the three most valuable calligraphic works housed here. These three treasures, most valued and adored by Emperor Qianlong (r. 1736-1795) of the Qing Dynasty (1616-1911), were *A Sunny Scene after a Quick Snow* by Wang Xizhi, *Mid-Autumn* by Wang Xianzhi and *Boyuan* by Wang Xun (349-400). As father and son, Wang Xizhi and Wang Xianzhi have been known as the "Two Wangs," their works universally recognized as the peak of Chinese calligraphy.

People set great value on Wang Xizhi's calligraphic works. They liken his handwriting to a "frolicking dragon," vigorous, yet refined and elegant. His *Preface to the Lanting Pavilion Collection*, known as a gem of Chinese calligraphy, was the most representative of his style.

This calligraphic masterpiece has been widely extolled by calligraphers throughout the ages, for its dynamic significance and extraordinary grace. However, all that remains extant today are facsimiles of the original – said to have been buried in

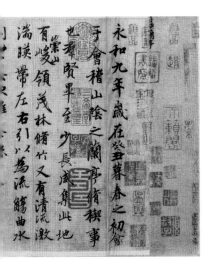

the tomb of Emperor Taizong (r. 627-649) of the Tang Dynasty, since he was so fond of it. Later generations were thus bereft of the chance to enjoy the genuine work. However, people's appreciation of it has nonetheless not been reduced. In fact, it has nurtured generations of calligraphers.

"Hidden Style" of the Yan Script

The Chinese people emphasize reserve in conduct and in calligraphic works as well. Being "hidden" is a requirement that a calligrapher must always bear in mind.

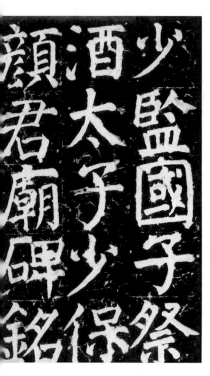

Inscription on the Tablet of the Yan Family Temple, by Yan Zhenqing (709-785): representative of the reserved yet evocative Yan Script

Yan Zhenqing (709-785) was a Tang-dynasty master calligrapher, renowned for his Yan-style writing. A beginner always starts learning with Yan-style calligraphy. As a young man, Yan Zhenqing once went to Zhang Xu for instruction. Zhang said to him, "When I started to learn calligraphy, I failed to make head or tail of it. One day, one of my friends and I were taking a walk down the banks of a river. Right at that moment, the water was crystal clear, the sand was gleaming clean, the white beach extended far into the distance beyond my eyesight, and I felt like writing. However, there was neither brush nor paper at hand. Fortunately, I had an iron awl with me, and I used this to write in the sand. The words, however, were quickly smoothed in half by the sand, leaving only some traces. It suddenly dawned on me: calligraphy is actually like words in the sand. The key point is 'being hidden!' It is in 'being hidden' that a calligraphic work becomes deep and rich in meaning, yet vigorous and powerful in style."

Yan Zhenqing had well grasped the meaning of the story, and "being hidden" became the highest criterion in his calligraphy. Based on this criterion, he developed the Yan style, which has had a far-reaching influence on the development of Chinese calligraphy as a whole. "Being hidden" means that, the beginning and end of each stroke are smooth, without any trace of sharp and overpowering brushwork.

Inscription on the Tablet of the Yan Family Temple is a masterpiece created in Yan Zhenqing's later years, which well reflects the characteristics of "being hidden." This work displays a calligraphic momentum in a reserved way; and represents Yan Zhenqing's highest achievement in calligraphy.

17. The Charm of Ink and Wash

Ink and wash is a unique genre of traditional Chinese painting. It uses little or no color but applies black ink in different shades to white paper or silk. Ink and wash is just as important in traditional Chinese painting as oils in European painting. A typical representative of traditional Chinese painting, it is one of the styles that best represent the spirit of China's fine arts.

Wang Wei (701-761), a famous Tang-dynasty (618-907) poet, is generally acknowledged as the first ink-and-wash painter in Chinese history. Yet what remains of his ink-and-wash work today is only a Northern-Song-dynasty (960-1127) copy of his *A Brook in the Snow* with his autograph. This painting depicts a brook in the wild, using no color but black ink, yet still incredibly reproducing a carefree, peaceful snowbound world. In the later half of the ninth century, that is, from the end of the Tang Dynasty through to the early Song Dynasty (960-1279), ink-and-wash painting gradually evolved as the main form in traditional Chinese painting, its influence reaching farther and wider than color painting. For a long time, the idea that "the ink and wash is supreme among all other styles of painting" has been the mainstream philosophy in traditional Chinese painting.

Black-and-White World

Apparently, the emergence and development of ink-and-wash painting is closely related to technology, materials and artistic traditions. Ink and wash is usually done on paper or silk, with paper being the main material. Chinese papermaking technology was highly developed, and different types of paper with fine textures and absorbent functions provided a solid foundation for the emergence of this painting genre. At the same time, the tradition of Chinese calligraphy exerted a direct influence on it. However, it was more the ideological factors – rather than the factors listed above – that were the main spur for its emergence and development.

A Brook in the Snow, by Wang Wei (701-761), Tang-dynasty poet and artist: reproduces a carefree, peaceful snowbound world.

Chinese artists have a special, fervent love for the black-and-white world featured simply with black ink on white paper or silk. A white-and-black world, to Chinese people, is a colorless world without bright, gorgeous colors. Chinese painting basically attached great importance to color. A good example is that, in the early days, paintings were called "red and green color" in China. Chinese artists used to advocate "applying color to depict color" – given the diversely colorful world, it is the artist's responsibility to reproduce the world with variegated colors. Yet the ink-and-wash painting triumphed over this tradition to become superior to all other genres of traditional Chinese fine arts.

Actually, in Chinese culture there has always been a cautious attitude toward very bright colors. If a person fixes his eyes on bright colors for a long time, he will be drawn into them and feel dizzy. Moreover, splendid colors can arouse people's desires and disturb their peace of mind. According to Chinese philosophy, external splendor and prosperity cannot necessarily represent the truth of the world. If one wants to know the real meaning of the world, one must look beyond superficial phenomena. These thoughts have directly affected the ways of artistic expression in Chinese painting – ink and wash replacing bright colors. "Extreme splendor ends in commonness" represents an important view in Chinese fine arts. The unadorned, common-looking black-and-white world well expresses people's yearning for a pure and simple world.

Chinese artists believe that "the use of ink can express the five colors" – the application of ink producing the feel of different colors, as well as feelings that color cannot convey. Dong Qichang (1555-1636), a famous Ming-dynasty (1368-1644) artist, once said to his students as he pointed to an ink-and-wash painting, "This is the most fascinating world." After the birth of ink and wash, Chinese paintings quickly broke away from seeking likeness in form. "The world through the eye" gave way to "the world through the mind," a practice that has become the common pursuit of Chinese artists.

Shaping Beyond Likeness ·

Ancient Chinese artists did not abide by the principle of perspective, and sometimes even tried to purposefully avoid the issue. From the 16th century onwards, many people have raised doubts and questions about this, the most representative of whom was Hendrik Willem Van Loon (1882-1944). He said, in his *The Art of Mankind*, that in this world, only the Chinese and children did not pay attention to the principle of perspective. He thus with scorn dismissed traditional Chinese painting.

China has boasted systematic books on art for over 1,500 years. Xie He (birth and death dates unknown), an art critic of the Southern Dynasties (420-589), put forward the "Six-way Theory," or six basic principles about painting, in his *Appreciating Classic Paintings* (*Guhua pinlu*). Among the six principles, "Vividly expressing flavor and tone" came first, and has remained the supreme principle for Chinese painting ever since. Over the long period of 1,500 years, flavor and tone in paintings have been much more stressed than likeness in form. Su Dongpo (1036-1101) of the Northern Song Dynasty said, "If one appreciates a painting from the perspective of resemblance, one's appreciation of art is level with children." This was a view quite contrary to Van Loon's. Van Loon remarked that the lack of the principle of perspective as well as likeness in form in Chinese paintings had kept them at the level of children's scrawls. Interestingly, Su Dongpo believed that if a person painted while bearing likeness in mind, he was no more than a child painting. What contradictory ideas European and Chinese artists held toward painting!

On the issue of perspective, there was once a heated debate in China. Wang Wei of the Tang Dynasty was an unconventional painter, who broke away from a fixed perspective when painting. He once drew different scenes of the four seasons in a single painting – *Yuan An Sleeping in the Snow*. In it, there is a scene of "a palm tree in the snow." It is an acknowledged fact that all palm leaves fall in the autumn and cannot possibly be seen in the icy cold winter. Some people make critical remarks on this, while more agree with the artist

A Scene of Forest after the Snow, *by Fan Kuan*
(birth and death dates unknown), Song Dynasty:
shows the freshness and ethereal ambience of
the forest after snow.

because they believed that to paint is to express feelings, not form; palm leaves in the snow are an image in the artist's mind, which can of course then be represented on the tableau.

There was indeed one Chinese painter who noticed the principle of perspective. He was the master landscape painter Li Cheng (919-967), from the early Northern Song Dynasty. He usually drew objects from a fixed point of view. For example, if he drew a building, he would stand at one point and look up at the eaves, and what he drew would be lifelike. However, Shen Kuo (1031-1095), a great scientist of the same dynasty, later made sharp criticisms of those paintings, believing that an artist should "look at the small from the perspective of the big," instead of the other way round as Li Cheng had done. That is to say, genuine artists should not focus on the specific details they see but should

A Scene of Early Spring, *by Guo Xi (1023-c. 1085), Northern Song Dynasty: captures through meticulous brushstrokes the seemingly warm but actually still cold spring.*

observe things with their "mind's eye." Artists should present the world in their mind, instead of being confined to what they physically see. This is what "looking at the small from the perspective of the big" means. "The big" here refers to the power of the human mind.

Chinese paintings depict an imagined world as well as a spiritual world. For instance, the Southern-Song-dynasty (1127-1279) artist Ma Yuan (1140-1225) once created a painting called *Angling Alone on the Cold River*. The scene is very simple, but the connotations of the painting are rich and profound. It features a tranquil night, with the moon shedding its pale light on the peaceful river, on which there is only one little boat. A man sits in the boat, his body slightly bent forward, his attention all focused on the water. The stern of the boat is turned slightly upwards, with faint traces of waves around it and a sense of leisure enveloping it, as it follows the water to wherever its flow may take it. Everything is painstakingly wrought to express a spiritual world free from worldly cares: a deep and serene night, cool and silent surroundings, a cold crescent moon, a little boat, and a lonely person, with this tranquil world all to himself. Apparently, the artist was not concerned with angling, but with the spiritual world he lived in. This is an important characteristic of Chinese painting.

The Rongxi Studio, *by Ni Yunlin (1301-1374), Yuan Dynasty: depicts a small hut set against the background of high mountains and a vast river, expressing the status of humans in the universe.*

A Lonely Bird, by Badashanren
(1626-1705), Qing Dynasty:
expresses the independent spirit
of the artist.

Landscape Painting of the Song and Yuan Dynasties

When people talk about Chinese landscape painting, they never fail to mention the landscape paintings of the Song and Yuan (1206-1368) dynasties. This period witnessed the maturity of ink-and-wash painting, when the techniques of ink and wash were applied to landscape painting, and thus brought Chinese painting to a zenith of prosperity and splendor. Master ink-and-wash landscape painters of this period include Dong Yuan (?-962), Ju Ran (birth and death dates unknown), Fan Kuan (birth and death dates unknown), Li Cheng, and Guo Xi (1023-c.1085), who helped develop the idea that a stretch of landscape represents a stretch of one's spiritual world, a tradition that emphasizes the representation of the human mind.

Ni Yunlin (1301-1374), Wu Zhen (1280-1354), Huang Gongwang (1269-1354), and Wang Meng (1308-1385) were the four foremost landscape painters of the Yuan Dynasty. Known as the "Four Masters of the Yuan," they all led hermit lives, enjoying the free clouds and green mountains of nature. They all advocated a free, natural and ethereal style in their paintings, so as to express a feeling of detachment with touches of indifference. And Ni Yunlin is considered the most typical of the four.

Ni's *The Rongxi Studio* employs a design of "a river and its two banks" for the tableau. At the lower part are a few bizarrely shaped rocks and several old withered trees. In the middle is an expanse of water; on the upper part, or the other side of the river, are mountains looming in the distance. Everything in the picture seems still: the water, the clouds, even the wind. There are no people strolling by, nor any fishing boats; only the lonely pavilion confronts the silent distant mountains; only the stagnant autumn river surrounds the secluded trees. It is a typical artistic conception of "cold mountains and thin waters."

In this painting, colors are completely abandoned and the "level and distant" method is applied to the composition of the painting, so as to achieve the effect of peace and detachment. The world created here is the world in the artist's mind: cold mountains and insignificant waters reveal the painter's desire to leave the earthly world; withered trees convey the artist's pursuit of freedom, though it means loneliness; the small pavilion under the seared trees is "Rongxi Studio," the name meaning a studio big enough only to hold

Bamboo and Rock, *by Zheng Banqiao (1693-1765), Qing Dynasty: portrays a sense of ease yet strength.*

a knee – a reflection of a human being's inferior position in the universe. The whole picture gives no sense of constriction but radiates with a peaceful atmosphere.

Innovation after the Ming and Qing Dynasties

The Ming and Qing (1616-1911) dynasties witnessed further development in ink-and-wash painting, in opposition to the traditions of the Song and Yuan dynasties. Artists expressed richer personal experiences and interests through ink and wash. Whereas landscape painting of the Northern Song Dynasty stood out for expression of momentum, and Yuan landscape painting for its expression of peaceful, detached ambience; artists in the Ming and Qing dynasties either emphasized expression of individual personality through intriguing brushwork, such as with Badashanren (alias of Zhu Da, 1626-1705) and Shi Tao (1630-1724), or focused on breaking through conventions to express the universe as they understood it, as in the "Eight Yangzhou Eccentric Painters," the most representative being Zheng Banqiao (1693-1765).

A Lonely Bird, a scroll painting by Badashanren, is an inspiring work. From the lower left side of the picture is a withered, slightly gnarled branch stretching upward and rightward, on the end of which is perched a pocketsize bird, its thin claws tightly clutching the branch. The bird's wings, half spread, and its eyes, small but calm, strikingly catch the viewer's attention. A withered twig and a lonely, single-eyed and single-footed bird – what a lonely world! Yet, how well it reflects the independent spirit of the artist!

Another representative work of Badashanren is *A Bird and Lotus*, done at the age of 67. This painting features a rootless lotus stem that stretches upward and rightward on the tableau, with a half-blooming bud. There is no pond to be seen, nor any lotus leaves. A bird flies from afar, seeming undecided whether to perch or not, so its perching with one thin claw on the stamen appears unsteady, its wings flapping in doubt, its eyes in a trance. All appears illusory and unsettled, through which the artist conveys his ideal of remaining aloof from the secular world.

Zheng Banqiao was a prestigious mid-Qing-dynasty artist of high artistic accomplishment. He excelled in painting orchids, bamboo and rocks. In his famous painting, *Ink Bamboo*, he created an elegant yet unrestrained composition, with a remarkably fresh atmosphere.

Ancient Chinese painters loved to paint plum, orchid, bamboo, and chrysanthemum, renowned in Chinese culture as the "four gentlemen." This is not because these plants are considered any better than the others, but they are believed to represent the character of human beings. It is with this in mind that Zheng Banqiao approached his bird-and-flower paintings. He said, "The bamboo is emaciated yet spirited, aloof yet proud, always reaching up toward the sky, never bending under the snow's attack – this is an unyielding spirit valued by the virtuous who never give in to worldly conventions. So, when I paint bamboo, I paint not only its image but also its spirit."

Ink-and-wash painting in the 20th century, while inheriting the strong points of traditional Chinese painting, also incorporated many innovations. A representative master was Qi Baishi (1864-1957), who excelled both in the ancient and modern arts. Based on what he learned from the style of Badashanren and Shi Tao, he expressed his own understanding and originality in

Shrimps, *by Qi Baishi (1864-1957): without showing water still successfully portrays a world of vibrant life.*

his works, especially his paintings of shrimps. Often he drew only one or two shrimps in a painting, leaving the rest of the tableau empty. This seemingly simple tableau, however, never fails to enchant viewers, as it always gives a feeling that everything in the painting is alive with an ethereal quality. One example is Qi's *Frogs Croaking out of the Stream*. With only a couple of swimming tadpoles in the painting, the artist vividly presents an animated world of a three-mile stream-a world full of life and vitality.

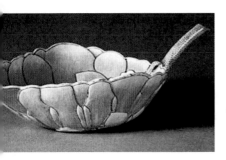

18. Porcelain — Calling Card of Chinese Culture

In English, the country and "porcelain" share the same name-"China." This proves that Europeans have long known of China's relationship to porcelain. Porcelain found its way to Europe in the 15th century, occupying an important position in the exchanges between China and other countries. The Keisel Randy Museum in Germany houses a blue-and-white bowl dating back to the Ming Dynasty (1368-1644). Throughout history, China, along with other Asian countries, and Europe maintained a busy and vast trade in porcelain. From 1602 to 1682, the Dutch East India Company transported more than 16 million articles of porcelain to Europe. Porcelain garnered a good reputation for China for its sophistication and elegance, and played an important role in the wave of the European idealization of China during the 17th and 18th centuries. In the rococo style popular in Europe of that time, one could sense, from time to time, the influence of "Chinese vogue" represented by China's styles of porcelain and gardens.

Porcelain is of great significance in the history of Chinese civilization. Pottery was the predecessor of porcelain, while glazed pottery was the basis for the emergence of porcelain. Around the first century, porcelain production first

Painted teacup with bird-and-flower design,
Chenghua reign (1465-1487),
Ming Dynasty

Bowl with floral design,
Xuande reign
(1426-1435), Ming
Dynasty

Bluish gray bowl with
sunflower-pattern rim,
Southern Song Dynasty

emerged in China, and by the Song Dynasty (960-1279) it had become mature. Song-dynasty porcelain represented the acme of Chinese porcelain technique. Five famous kilns, the Jun, Ding, Guan, Ge, and Ru, were all creative and original in their respective products, and their porcelain ware has been imitated by later generations throughout the ages. In the Yuan Dynasty (1206-1368), Jingdezhen became the center of the Chinese porcelain industry.

Chinese porcelain is cherished for its serene color, crystal paste, graceful designs, and ingenious forms-a quest of generations of craftspeople. Bronzeware, pottery and porcelain are all popular with the Chinese people, though their styles vary widely. Pottery is simple and unsophisticated, while bronzeware suggests solemnity, but porcelain is the most exquisite and elegant.

Porcelain can be regarded as the calling card of Chinese culture. This calling card represents the crystallization of Chinese culture and the embodiment of the aesthetic pursuits of the Chinese people.

Nature's Craft

Anyone familiar with Chinese porcelain knows that the surface of some porcelain ware is covered with irregular cracks. This is referred to as "crackling" in porcelain terminology. The crackles occurred during kilning due to flawed workmanship, but as time went on crackleware became a craze during the Song Dynasty, and was passed down to this very day. Crackleware today is one of the typical Chinese porcelain styles.

The Ge Kiln (located in present-day Longquan, Zhejiang Province) was a typical kiln of the Song Dynasty that produced crackleware. Today, the Shanghai Museum has two pieces of crackleware from this kiln. One is a bowl with its rim shaped in a sunflower pattern, and the other a bowl with its rim shaped in a floral pattern. Both of them have fine crisscrossing crackles on the surface. The Taipei Palace Museum has a piece of crackleware produced in the Ge Kiln of the Yuan Dynasty. It is an incense burner with fish-shaped handles. Thin and fine crackles on the cream-colored glaze are evocative of a tree leaf, with arteries and veins stretching, intertwined freely and vibrantly in it.

Chinese people love crackleware because they love nature's unique craft. Porcelain is an artificial art, but what it most defies is nothing other than artificiality. The interest in crackleware lies in its naturally produced and unpredictable patterns. Any manmade crackles would be mechanical and unnatural and betray a certain artifice, definitely no match for naturally crafted crackles.

Incense burner with fish-shaped handles,
Yuan Dynasty

Celadon bowl,
Southern Song Dynasty

Plate with flowers-of-four-seasons design, Xuande reign (1426-1435), Ming Dynasty

Blue-and-white porcelain plate, Yongle reign (1403-1424), Ming Dynasty

Pure Blue-and-White Porcelain

Pure and elegant beauty is the goal that porcelain pursues, and this ideal is best explained in the production of blue-and-white porcelain.

Blue-and-white porcelain is a typical artifact of porcelain in China. Among the porcelain exported during the Ming and Qing (1616-1911) dynasties, 80 percent was blue-and-white. Chinese-made blue-and-white porcelain ware emerged long before the founding of the Tang Dynasty (618-907), but it was not until the Yuan Dynasty that this type of porcelain came to be produced in quantity, with the attendant masterpieces. The Ming Dynasty witnessed the maturity of the art, and a large number of valuable pieces were produced in this period. Jingdezhen, a small town that created the enchanting blue-and-white porcelain of the Yuan Dynasty, became its porcelain-producing center; and in the subsequent Ming Dynasty, the imperial kilns were established here. Blue-and-white porcelain is now the most representative of Chinese porcelain.

To produce blue-and-white porcelain, cobalt oxide is requisite. It is employed to draw on the white roughcast before glaze is applied. After kilning at a high temperature, the roughcast turns into blue-and-white porcelain, since cobalt oxide turns blue with heat. The white surface with blue patterns and a shiny sheen of glaze produces a pure, elegant and transparent effect.

In the Taipei Palace Museum there is a bowl with branch-and-flower pattern, produced in the Xuande reign (1426-1435) of the Ming Dynasty. Its shape demonstrates a primitive simplicity, while its fine texture is white with a touch of blue. In a well-balanced composition, the flowers are vividly drawn with soft and serene lines, while the blue intermingles with the white, producing a harmonious, effervescent effect.

The Taipei Palace Museum houses another piece of blue-and-white porcelain ware – a plate with a flowers-of-four-seasons design, also made in the Xuande reign of the Ming Dynasty. The interior of the plate features 13 flowers, including chrysanthemum, lotus, gardenia, pomegranate, Chinese herbaceous peony, hibiscus, and camellia; while its exterior is decorated with several flowers. In the center of the plate sits the lotus – the divine flower of Buddhism and a commonly used motif in Chinese porcelain. The white plate looks crystal clear, and although the designs are complicated, the pure white color and the graceful blue match each other, to produce an elegant, sophisticated effect.

Blue-and-white porcelain occupies a prominent position in the Chinese porcelain industry, for it accords well with the culture and aesthetic spirit Chinese people have long pursued – of simplicity, unaffectedness and ease.

Chinese people believe that ultimate beauty is simple and natural; anything that is affected and over-polished runs contradictory to this philosophy. As representative of Chinese porcelain, blue-and-white porcelain displays a world of conciseness and elegance, serenity and purity. Blue and white form a single-color painting, which may appear monotonous but this is the exact feature of blue-and-white porcelain, free of excessive decoration or exaggeration. Blue-and-white porcelain also seeks an effect of transparency, which was achieved in the products made in the official kilns of the Yuan and Ming dynasties. These products boast a thin, transparent white paste set off by blue designs,

*Underglaze red vase,
Hongwu reign (1368-1398),
Ming Dynasty*

*Underglaze red
decanter, Hongwu
reign, Ming Dynasty*

which are clean and clear and convey a sense of loftiness and unearthliness.

A Subtle and Reserved World

Most Chinese porcelain ware embodies the characteristics of Confucian aesthetics. In its pursuit of gentleness and refinement one senses the aesthetic propensities of Confucianism; through its implicit and reserved artistic style one discovers the reserved nature of Confucian aesthetics.

The Song Dynasty was a renaissance period for Confucianism, and also a period of maturity in porcelain production. This was much more than a simple coincidence. The increased popularity of Confucianism advanced the remarkable development of Song-dynasty porcelain production, while its aesthetic standards gave enlightenment to porcelain craftspeople. The tradition of Song-dynasty porcelain— emphasizing internal beauty – has been observed by generation after generation, and its reserved style has made the art of Chinese porcelain thought-provoking while pleasing to the eye.

Another representative of a reserved style is underglaze red porcelain, one of the two types of porcelain developed to its maturity in Jingdezhen during the Yuan Dynasty. Difficult to produce, underglaze red is not as popular as blue-and-white porcelain, though it displays a high artistic taste.

A precious underglaze red vase, produced during the Hongwu reign (1368-1398) of the Ming Dynasty, is now housed in the Taipei Palace Museum. Its design is drawn in underglaze red, and at the lower section is a circular design of lotus petals. Palm trees, rocks and groves of bamboo, drawn on the belly of the vase, produce a graceful landscape painting with profound allusions.

Pale greenish blue plate shaped like a chrysanthemum flower, Southern Song Dynasty

Shape and Imagery

Porcelain is a comprehensive art, and form is as important to a good piece of porcelain as it is to a fine piece of sculpture. For porcelain ware of artistic value, an intriguing shape can capture instant attention from viewers.

Among Chinese porcelain, there is a type of white porcelain decorated with floral patterns of the same color, which suggests a feeling of relief sculpture. The most famous white porcelain was produced in the Ding Kiln of the Song Dynasty, which exerted a great influence on later white porcelain products. A small white porcelain container produced during the Qing Dynasty's Daoguang reign (1821-1850) is such a piece in the white series. From the exterior, it looks no different from an ordinary container for holding go (a board game) pieces, but on the interior are relief-like flowers with five-color petals concisely and elegantly outlined. It must have been a great delight to enjoy this exquisitely made artwork while playing go!

Celadon teacup, Yuan Dynasty

Chinese porcelain also pursues painting effects. Porcelain ware usually contains images from landscapes as well as bird-and-flower paintings. Most porcelain craftspeople were also adept at painting. For Ming- and Qing-dynasty porcelain ware, elegance in shape, intriguing use of color, fine texture, and vivid images all set off each other, adding great splendor to the art.

Under the influence of European painting, at the end of the Ming Dynasty and the beginning of the Qing Dynasty, Chinese porcelain began to incorporate European artistic techniques into its design, such as through the use of light and shadow, to make the whole design vivid with three-dimensional effects. A fine example is the *famille-rose* porcelain that was popular in the Qing Dynasty.

Famille-rose, also referred to as "soft-color," was so named as to differentiate it from the application of color without shading changes. The *famille-rose* vase with nine-peach design, a Qing-dynasty work now housed in the Beijing Palace Museum, employs the *famille-rose* method, instead of the traditional repetitively used five colors. It pays attention to changing color shades as well as light and shadow, producing vivid, three-dimensional effects with a strong realistic flavor.

19. Gardens South of the Yangtze River

Chinese people started to build gardens more than 2,000 years ago. Over this long period of time, three styles of gardens came into being: the imperial garden, the temple garden and the private garden. Among them, the most famous imperial garden extant today is the Summer Palace in Beijing, while the private gardens south of the lower reaches of the Yangtze River boast a unique ambience of their own. Scattered through Suzhou, Yangzhou and other places, the private gardens are mostly legacies from the Ming (1368-1644) and Qing (1616-1911) dynasties. Each resembling a landscape painting, they are of unmatched charm.

A Winding Path to Places of Interest

The Chinese attach great importance to the qualities of being reserved and subtle, and the construction of gardens dotting the hazy landscape south of the lower Yangtze River well reflects this philosophy. The pavilions and buildings enshrouded in the misty moonlight produce an irresistible appeal.

Round gate in Canglang Pavilion Garden, Suzhou

In the gardens, besides buildings looming behind dense groves of trees, what most frequently meets the eye are winding paths that seemingly lead to nowhere, as it would appear to new visitors. There, a path seems to end, but all of a sudden, a new world is rolled out before you: pavilions, rock formations, spring water – all combining to provide a pleasant surprise!

At the entrance to a Chinese garden there is usually a huge stone or wall to screen your view. The most typical example is the Summer Palace. When you enter the eastern gate, a big hall blocks your way. This is to give you a pressed-in feeling, so as to later produce unforeseen delight when you turn around the hall to see the exotic rock formations, and an extensive lake of limpid rippling water right in front of you.

Private gardens south of the Yangtze River are a world of curving lines. In Zhuozheng Garden in Suzhou, corridors zigzag along a stream, only to be interrupted at intervals by pavilions partly overhanging the water. The upturned corners of the roofs are like flying birds with their wings widespread, giving a sense of motion to a still picture. Even the trees are curving: the weeping willows with branches cascading down to touch the water; ancient trees of hundreds of years with gnarling old branches; numerous dragon-claw trees, entwining vines, and plum trees with beautifully arched sparse branches. All proclaim the beauty of this curving world.

Fascinating Stones

Rock formations play an important role in the construction of a Chinese-style garden. Without them, a garden could not be considered an authentic Chinese-style

House amid
bamboo groves

Guanyun Peak in Liuyuan Garden, Suzhou

garden. Western tourists may find that in a Chinese-style garden there are no sculptures – as often seen in a European garden. Actually, rock formations are as important to a Chinese-style garden as sculptures are to a European-style garden, and may signify even more.

Guanyun Peak, in Liuyuan Garden in Suzhou, is actually a formation of stones from Taihu Lake. It stands near a spring, its shadow reflecting clearly in the water. The rock formation is modeled after a peak in real life. Between the reality and the reflection, the garden presents a fascinating, picturesque composition. At the foot of the rock formation are delicate yellow, white or red flowers, and halfway up the peak a pavilion alights; upwards is the peak pointing at the sky. From the bottom of the water to the water surface, the foot of the rock formation, the halfway view, and the sky, all constitute a landscape of rich layers of different views, and this is the very essence of a southern garden: the detail making for a perfect garden.

Taihu Lake stones are precious materials frequently used in the building of artificial hills in gardens south of the Yangtze River. People value them for their thinness, porosity, exquisiteness, as well as wrinkles. Thinness represents unearthliness and aloofness; porosity signifies openness and flexibility, which allows for the free flow of energy; exquisiteness describes the characteristics of being fine and delicate in texture, like jade; while wrinkles are the curving forms and ripple-like lines nurtured by water. These four features of Taihu Lake stones describe not only beauty in form but even more, reflect people's lofty ideals toward life.

A Sense of Space

Gardens in the south are mostly small in size. To evoke a sense of space, the

Window in a garden south of the lower Yangtze River

use of "borrowing a distant view" is of special significance. It enables a visitor to look outside the garden to enjoy a new and greater vista, and to acquire a feeling of spaciousness, despite being in a physically small space.

Windows are very important in this aspect. In Chinese horticulture, windows are always designed in the shape of a fan and referred to as "convenience windows." Through the windows, visitors can view the picturesque bamboo groves and mountains outside. Joyous Longevity Hall, in the Summer Palace in Beijing, has windows on all its four walls, with its surrounding walls facing Kunming Lake. Each window view becomes the equivalent of a vivid painting. In fact, garden designers bestow these windows with another name - "absorbent windows," through which the sights of different places interact, thus setting the landscape of the garden in motion. More interestingly, through the windows,

A corner of Yipu Garden in Suzhou, with white stones and a red tree setting each other off

An undulating wall in Xiyuan Garden, Suzhou

visitors may see different views at different angles, and thus the composition of the garden becomes infinitely enlarged.

The idea of "borrowing a distant view" is actually applied not only to windows, but also to all the elements of the garden, such as houses, pavilions and pagodas. A horizontal board in the Summer Palace bears the inscription, "The colors of the mountain and the light of the lake gather in this building." This is saying that the building has absorbed a panoramic view of the landscape all around, a good example of "borrowing a distant view."

Pavilions are an integrated part of Chinese gardens. Their function is to divert visitors' attention from a view in a limited space toward a view out into an infinite space. Standing in a pavilion, a visitor can look far into the distance to enjoy the beautiful sights of the world. As a Yuan-dynasty (1206-1368) poem elucidates, *"The boundless landscape / Converges into one pavilion."* In the Summer Palace in Beijing, there is a pavilion named "Touring Through a Painting," which does not mean that the pavilion itself is a painting, but that the scene outside the pavilion is like a painting. Therefore, once you enter the pavilion, you enter the bigger painting.

A glimpse of Zhuozheng Garden: white walls and black tiles amidst a stretch of green

The Canglang Pavilion Garden in Suzhou is famous for its pavilion. Atop a hill, the Canglang Pavilion seems to have the ability to command winds and clouds. Inside the pavilion, visitors capture a bird's-eye-view of the beautiful scenery all around and below. A couplet inscribed on the pillars of the pavilion reads, "Invaluable are the gentle breeze and the bright moon; lovable are the distant mountains and the nearby rivers." Sitting in the pavilion and enjoying "the distant mountains and the nearby rivers" can soothe the souls of visitors – the ideal of Chinese landscapists.

To enhance a sense of space, Chinese garden designers have adopted a variety of methods to arrange, organize and create space, such as "borrowing scenery," "dividing scenery," "separating scenery," and even "borrowing scenery with a mirror."

"Borrowing scenery" is one of the basic principles that Chinese landscapists generally adopt. For example, the pagoda atop Jade Spring Mountain appears to be part of the landscape of the Summer Palace; from the Guanyun Building in

Suzhou's Liuyuan Garden, one can enjoy the scenery of Tiger Hill Park in the distance; the Liangyi Pavilion built on an artificial hill in Zhuozheng Garden commands a beautiful landscape outside the garden's wall. All these are good examples of "borrowing scenery," and all of them successfully break through the barrier of walls to integrate inward the landscapes outside.

Actually, the names of many buildings in Chinese gardens reflect this principle of "borrowing scenery," such as "Smoke and Rain Hall," "Hall for Listening to the Rain," "Moon and Wind Pavilion," "Lotus and Wind Pavilion," and "Flying Fountain Pavilion," to name only a few. These names suggest that these sites function to bring natural landscapes closer for the appreciation of visitors.

The Long Corridor in the Summer Palace divides the landscape into two parts: one being the natural beauty of Kunming Lake; the other, the architectural complex representing human interests. A visitor enjoys the different scenery on the two sides at the same time; this is called "dividing scenery."

A fine example of the application of the principle "separating scenery" is the Harmony Garden in the Summer Palace. It is a garden within a garden, that is, an independent space in itself yet also a space dependent on a larger one. Chinese landscapists excel at using this theory because they believe that the more separated a space is, the more spacious it becomes, and the richer the feelings it evokes in visitors.

Hanging a mirror opposite a window to absorb the outside scenery is called "borrowing scenery with a mirror." By using this method, the real world turns into a virtual world. A pool or lake in a garden also serves this purpose.

To summarize, whatever the methods used, every effort is made to achieve the purpose of giving visitors a sense of space in the garden. This is an important and specialized field to understand, if one wants to truly appreciate Chinese aesthetics.

20. Peking Opera:
Artistry of Performers

Many foreign friends first learn about Chinese culture through the numerous Chinese restaurants found all over the world, and soon discern that China is a country with delicious cuisine. The second impression of Chinese culture is often Peking Opera, whose masks are now almost emblematic of China. Many countries design posters using Peking Opera masks to signal a "Year of Chinese Culture." To understand Chinese culture, therefore, some knowledge about Peking Opera is indeed indispensable.

The Delights of Peking Opera Masks

China's Peking Opera radiates with the beauty of resplendent color – vivid, intense and glamorous. This artistic beauty comes not only from the costumes but also from the masks of exaggerated, dazzling designs, gleaming with reds, purples, whites, yellows, blacks, blues, greens, every diverse color imaginable.

Masks, applied to the two roles of the "*jing*" or "male character" and the "*chou*" or "clown" serve two purposes. One is to indicate the identity and character of the role. For example, a "red face" means the person is loyal and brave; a "black face" signifies the person is straightforward; and a "white face" identifies the person as crafty and evil. The other purpose is to express people's appraisal of the roles from a moral and aesthetic point of view, such as respectable, hateful, noble, or ridiculous, etc.

Besides being evocative, Peking Opera masks are in and of themselves an art of beautiful colors and designs for aesthetic appreciation. For example, Zhang Fei, a heroic character from the Three Kingdoms Period (220-280), has a facial design in Peking Opera in the shape of a butterfly – a masterpiece perfectly combining personality and artistic design. The intriguing beauty of the color and design of Peking Opera masks adds to the attractive spectacle onstage. Many Chinese folk handicrafts (e.g., kites, dough and clay figurines, carpets, tapestries), posters, advertisements, and fashions adopt Peking Opera masks as a source element in their designs.

Peking Opera Performance: Sing, Speak, Act, and Fight

To Chinese people, going to the theater to enjoy Peking Opera or other artistic performances is known as "seeing plays." What is a "play" in the Chinese context? In Peking Opera, "a play" is not so much the story or plot but a world of images created onstage, a wonderful arena of harmony between sentiments and settings.

Zhang Fei, a hero in the Peking Opera Reed Pond

The "play" or "world of images" created by Peking Opera naturally relies on the plot provided by the script, and more importantly on the performance of the actors. However, to form a "world of images" in Peking Opera, the plot of a story provides only the framework and background, while the charm is produced by the actors' performances. Mei Lanfang (1894-1961), the greatest Peking Opera artist, once remarked that the feature of the art of Peking Opera is "actors being at the center." Peking Opera actors are the crux in creating a world of images onstage.

Dou Erdun in the Peking Opera Stealing an Imperial Horse

The performance of a Peking Opera actor can be summarized into four basic aspects, of singing, speaking, acting, and fighting, the core of which is a combination of song and choreography.

Singing is of utmost importance in the performance of Peking Opera, because first of all, Peking Opera is a singing art. Any famous Peking Opera boasts several wonderful arias that are well known and popular with audiences. The charm of the melodies usually embodies the sublime realm of the art of Peking Opera. Unable to appreciate the magic of Peking Opera arias, one would fail to enjoy the profound beauty of the art itself.

God Erlang in the Peking Opera Monkey King Wreaking Havoc on the Heavenly Court

Speaking refers to character monologues and dialogues, which serve to propel the development of the story. Speaking, like singing, needs to be executed in an appealing way.

The splendor of Peking Opera costumes

Acting and fighting mean that actors employ physical movements to express the emotions of the characters and the circumstances. Acting includes body movements and eye movements, solo dancing or group dancing, etc. Most of the dancing is choreographed movements from everyday life. Fighting is choreographed martial arts and acrobatics to depict fight or battle scenes. As the art of Peking Opera depends on movement to depict events, actors are given much room to perform on the stage. In the opera *Picking up the Jade Bracelet*, the young woman Sun Yujiao and the young scholar fall in love with each other, their eyes affixed on each other as if a thread connected them. Then, as Matchmaker Liu uses her pipe to pull the "virtual" line up and down, the young couple's eyes accordingly move up and down. These actions produce great humor and add much significance to the performance. Acting and fighting serve the whole "play" or the "world of images," but at the same time they are themselves a beautiful art in both form and skill. For example, in *King Chu Bids Farewell to His Concubine*, artist Mei Lanfang performed a sword dance in a miraculously skillful way, which became very popular with audiences. This is a type of beauty in form. As for the beauty of skill, this usually includes some very difficult acrobatic movements, often referred to as "superb skills."

The uniqueness of performances in Peking Opera lies in the fact that the singing, speaking, acting, and fighting, all focus on one or two actors in the play.

These performers used to be called "*jue'er*," hence "*mingjue*" was used to refer to famous actors or actresses. In this sense, the world of imagery created in Peking Opera mainly relies on the singing, speaking, acting, and fighting of actors, especially in the performance of the famous plays. This is the biggest difference between Peking Opera and other forms of performing arts in terms of aesthetic appreciation. And the remark – "Peking Opera is the art of performers" – well describes its quintessence.

The art of Peking Opera has a history of more than 200 years, and the practice and experience of countless Peking Opera artists prove that the aesthetic beauty of the art lies in none other than this fact.

The Beauty of a "Virtual World"

Depicting a "virtual world" is a distinctive feature of Peking Opera. Its virtuality consists of two aspects: one is virtual movements, and the other virtual settings. Virtual movement refers to imitating actions onstage. For example, riding a horse. Onstage, an actor cannot ride a real horse, but can only hold a whip and imitate the movement of galloping by walking around the stage, turning the body, wielding

Peking Opera performers onstage

the whip, and pulling the reins. A virtual setting means creating an imagined environment onstage. For example, rowing a boat. As there is no water or boat on the stage, an actor usually takes an oar and, through actions, makes the audience "see" the rowing of a boat on water.

The setting of the stage is very simple. Usually there is only one table and two chairs. The table, besides functioning as a table, may also symbolize a bed when an actor acts asleep by sitting at it with one hand upon it propping up his head. If he stands on the table and looks into the distance, it turns into a city gate tower. Simply put, changes in the stage setting follow the performance of the actors.

The effectiveness of virtual movements and virtual settings lies in their giving prominence to the actors' performances, helping the audience feel the rich connotations of the opera and its infinite appeal. Let us take two highlights from two operas as examples.

One is *At the Crossroad*. This opera describes the story of two *yamen* runners escorting Jiao Zan to prison. On the way they stay at an inn for the night. Ren Tanghui, whose task is to protect Jiao Zan, checks in at the same time. The owner of the inn, however, suspects Ren Tanghui is planning to murder Jiao Zan, so he gropes his way into Ren's room at night. Thus a fight starts. What is special about the performance is that, although the fight happens at night, the stage is brightly lit; yet the audience is able to sense it is a pitch-dark night from the actors' performances, which feature stealthy movements typical of people in darkness. Sometimes, one man's sword swishes down, only a few inches away from the other's face, yet the latter feels nothing, thus producing a breathtaking yet meaningful and humorous effect.

The other example is *Autumn River*, a play transplanted from Sichuan Opera. This story describes a young nun, Chen Miaochang who leaves the nunnery to pursue her lover Pan Bizheng. Onstage, there is neither water nor boat, but through the performance of the young woman and the old boatman, the audience is able to obviously "see" that the stage is a river. The boat sways forward; all the way there the girl complains about the boat for being slow, while the old boatman keeps teasing her about her anxiety to see her lover. The performance is full of wit and humor.

These examples describe the function of the "virtual world" in the art of Peking Opera, which provides limitless room for the performances of actors; and in return, performers present the audience with a world of images full of appealing wit. If in fact the stage of *At the Crossroad* was really all black to represent the dark night, and there was a real boat on the stage of *Autumn River*, what could the actors do? And would we still find as much wit and meaning in the performances? We doubt it.

"Watching a Play Is Watching Famous Actors"

Among audiences of Peking Opera there is a popular saying, "Watching a play is watching famous actors," or "Listening to an opera is listening to famous performers singing." Such remarks aptly summarize the foremost of the main features of appreciating Peking Opera.

The features of appreciating Peking Opera are decided by the characteristics of image creation in Peking Opera.

Viewers of Peking Opera go to the theater with the purpose of not only seeing "a play," but more of watching the "performance," since they know the "play" (or stage imagery) is to be "acted out," and the significance of the "play" is located in the singing, speaking, acting, and fighting of the performers. When enjoying an opera, they bear in mind not only the protagonists of the story but also the performers who play the roles. And the performances of the actors are what they have come to the theater to enjoy, especially when the performers are well known. This is the meaning of "Watching a play is watching famous actors."

Stage depiction of an old man in Peking Opera

Stage depiction of young women in Peking Opera

Another observation from Peking Opera audiences is that, "the more familiar an opera, the more enjoyable." Watching a film once may be enough, since watching it again usually lacks the excitement and joy felt the first time. However, when a person watches a vignette of Peking Opera, the more one is familiar with it, the further the background and plot of the story recede into the distance, and the more one focuses on enjoying the performances of the actors, and feels, grasps and enjoys the deeper meaning and magic of the actors' performances.

The second characteristic of Peking Opera appreciation is that the audience always separates the beauty of the craft and form of the performance from the world of imagery. A short aria or acrobatic movement will win admiring applause from the audience. Yet this is different from enjoying a film or a play. Usually, when the audience see a person performing stunts in a film or play, they never applaud this because they only see the role; in Peking Opera, however, the same scene may bring the house down, because theatergoers pay attention to both the role and the actor, and to the beauty in form and skill of the actor's performance.

As the famous German dramatist Bertolt Brecht (1898-1956) once remarked, when we watch a Chinese actor perform onstage, we see at least three characters at the same time: one being the performer (the actor), and also the two roles being performed (the actor and the role). He thus calls performance in Peking Opera a "dual performance," an important feature in the appreciation of Peking Opera. From the "dual performance," different audiences appreciate different aspects. Some prefer the entire role-centered imagery on the stage, while others enjoy the performance of the actor (this kind of audience usually listen to the singing with their eyes closed); and most shift between the two, gaining double enjoyment from the "dual performance."

Mei Lanfang, Great Peking Opera Artist

In the history of Peking Opera, there have arisen many celebrated performers, including certain legendary artists of great accomplishment. Mei Lanfang is a worthy exemplar.

Mei Lanfang was an actor who played the role of young women (*dan*). Together with Cheng Yanqiu (1904-1958), Shang Xiaoyun (1900-1976) and Xun Huisheng (1900-1968), they were acclaimed the "four famed Peking Opera female-role performers." Mei Lanfang had a melodious voice, a beautiful stage appearance, with elegant dancing and movements onstage. He crafted a noble and natural image, reaching the zenith of female-role performance. Mei Lanfang made innovations to the art of Peking Opera in different aspects. He composed many new melodies, introduced facial expressions, movements and the technique of dancing to the accompaniment of singing, from Kunqu Opera to Peking Opera; he also created various dances, such as the silk dance, sword dance, sleeve dance, and duster dance. He was the first to use the *erhu* to support the *jinghu* (traditional stringed instruments), to accompany singing by the female role, thus musically enriching Peking Opera. He also made innovations to masks, hairstyles and costumes. His representative operas include *The Drunken Concubine*, *King Chu Bids Farewell to His Concubine*, *The Universe*, and *Woman General Mu Guiying*.

Mei Lanfang's appearance, costumes, dance, movements, and singing onstage are all extremely striking. *The Drunken Concubine* depicts a woman's graceful appearance and conduct in an inebriated state. *The Universe* describes a woman named Zhao Yanrong pretending to have gone mad, who yet presents a beautiful image despite her insanity. Mei Lanfang's performances fully demonstrated Chinese classical beauty with everlasting allure. He is worthy of the title of "master artist of Peking Opera."

Mei Lanfang headed several delegations on performance tours to the United States, Japan and European countries, winning an international reputation for Peking Opera.

Mei Lanfang performing onstage in his later years

21. A Variety of Splendid Folk Arts

Folk arts in China have developed dynamically, with many forms enjoying a worldwide reputation. Here we present an introduction to a select few.

Cloisonné: Artifacts with the Gleam of Precious Gems

Cloisonné is a traditional art widely known in and outside China. It is a kind of superb local expertise from Beijing, which combines the skills of bronze art, porcelain, carving, and other types of folk arts. It is deemed valuable in the eyes of collectors, as well as providing refined ornaments for daily use.

A Qing-dynasty (1616-1911) cloisonné vase with a peach-and-bat design is a famous artifact. Its mouth, belly and base are welded together instead of being originally one piece. Its surface is first inlaid with copper wires, before the colorful glaze is applied. The nine peaches and bats have the symbolic meaning of happiness, longevity and peace.

The making of cloisonné first appeared during the Jingtai reign (1450-1457) of the Ming Dynasty (1368-1644), with the main color used being blue, hence the name "Jingtai blue" or cloisonné as it became known later on. By the time of the Chenghua reign (1465-1487), the techniques for making cloisonné were further developed, with products of this period looking heavy and dignified yet not lacking in eloquence or vividness. Its cast was always made of choice copper, decorated with enamel and colorful glaze naturally extracted from minerals, so that it would resemble precious gems. The Ming cloisonné artifacts extant today were mostly produced during the Jingtai and Chenghua reigns.

Cloisonné production involves very complicated techniques, with more than 30 working procedures. First, the making of the copper cast: plates of copper are tapped into a certain form, and fixed through firing at high temperatures. Then craftspeople use nippers to apply hair-thin copper wires onto the surface of the cast to form various designs. This technique is called "filigree." The concave designs are then filled with enamel and glaze of different colors, a technique known as "stippling blue." After being fired at high temperatures, the enamel and glaze coagulate, and careful burnishing is then needed. With the final touches of gilding, a cloisonné product is finished.

Cloisonné was further developed during the Qing Dynasty. Technically, while it overcame the weakness of the porosity of the Ming products, but artistically, it lacked the former's simplicity and dignified heaviness. After the Qing Dynasty, due to overproduction and the uneven skills of craftspeople, the quality of cloisonné could hardly match that of Ming cloisonné products.

New Year Pictures: Enhancing the Festive Atmosphere

Spring Festival (or Chinese New Year) is the most important traditional festival in China. People celebrate it with lanterns and streamers, no matter where they live, in the countryside or in the city. New Year pictures are an indispensable part of this celebration for each and every household. People put up New Year pictures in their homes to enhance the lively festive atmosphere.

Most New Year pictures feature designs symbolizing good fortune, auspiciousness and festivity. A popular New Year picture entitled *Surplus in Successive Years* depicts a cute plump baby holding a big carp in his arms and a bouquet of lotus flowers in his hand. "Fish" and "surplus" in Chinese have the same pronunciation (*yu*). Through the homophony of the two words, people express their wishes for affluent lives.

China is a country of vast territory, so the styles of New Year pictures vary from north to south. The northern New Year pictures are best represented by those produced in Yangliuqing in Tianjin Municipality, while in the south there are those from Taohuawu in Suzhou City, Jiangsu Province.

Yangliuqing New Year picture:
Mother and Sons Playing

Yangliuqing is a small town located in the southwestern outskirts of Tianjin. About 300 years ago, its New Year pictures began to enjoy great fame, with every family adept at creating this particular genre of painting. Yangliuqing New Year pictures adopt the method of xylograph overprinting combined with hand-painted color, hence establishing its distinctive feature of "half printing, half painting." The process goes like this: 1) carve designs out of wood; 2) print the pictures; 3) color the pictures; and 4) mount the pictures. All pictures are handmade paintings rather than mass-produced products, and all evoke traces of the woodcut and the feel of brushwork. With exquisite craftsmanship, Yangliuqing New Year pictures are very popular with Chinese people.

The lively festive atmosphere is best reflected in the Yangliuqing New Year pictures. Fresh and effervescent, each picture reproduces an interesting scene from everyday life. For example, *Mother and Son* depicts a lakeside courtyard, inside which are rock formations and flowers. The mother stands at a window, fan in hand, calling out to her son frolicking outside. The plump son in a bellyband holds a wooden stick with a bird perching on it. The whole picture brims with an affectionate, loving atmosphere of family life.

Yangliuqing New Year picture: Mother and Son

Taohuawu New Year pictures, produced using traditional techniques of watercolor block printing, are characteristic of the delicate and gentle style in areas south of the lower reaches of the Yangtze River. Thematically, the pictures draw much from the paintings of literati as well as folk stories; while artistically, most are scholarly and refined, unlike the heavy and resplendent style of the Yangliuqing pictures. Taohuawu New Year pictures once spread to Japan and exerted a certain influence on Japanese ukiyoe paintings, or paintings from the "floating world". About 300 years ago, Taohuawu New Year pictures began learning from the style of Western bronze carvings, as well as the use of shadow. Celebrated for its pure and attractive images of women,

Taohuawu New Year pictures enjoy great popularity among the Chinese people.

Papercuts: a World Created with Scissors

The papercut is a special folk art in China, with a history of nearly 1,000 years. The materials used are simple: ordinary paper and a pair of scissors (or a cutting knife). A skilled paper-cutting craftsperson cuts paper into designs like doing magic tricks. A piece of red paper is folded and then cut several times, before being unfolded into an attractive picture. Some craftspeople do not even set their eyes on what they are doing; they can even place a piece of paper inside a baggy sleeve and cut it into a beautiful pattern. Papercutting is a type of improvised art with powerful expression: a papercut artist does not need a model picture to copy from, but relies on a pair of scissors to produce a work of art, each time with slight differences. Papercuts are very popular in rural areas.

In the city of Xi'an, Shaanxi Province, people once used paper instead of glass as window-covering. As white paper was monotonous and considered inauspicious, clever and deft young women started to cut pieces of red paper into joyous baby images or beautiful butterflies, which they put on the windows to add liveliness to ordinary windows.

Two folk papercuts

In ancient China, people enjoyed the tradition of making and hanging lanterns for festivals and joyous occasions. The shapes of lanterns varied, from red lanterns hung in midair, running-horse lanterns, lotus lanterns on the surface of water, and lion lanterns loved by children. People sometimes drew pictures on the lanterns but more often would prefer to paste papercuts of different patterns, which, set off by the lantern light, became even more vivid and interesting.

Embroidery: Ten Fingers Like a Spring Breeze

China is home to silk and to a variety of arts related to silk, one of which is embroidery. Most embroiderers are women, hence the byname for embroidery of, "women's needlework." With a long history of several thousand years, embroidery has been a love of the Chinese people. It is applied to adorn clothes, quilts and pillowcases, or a piece of embroidery work can be an ornament in itself.

As early as in the Song Dynasty (960-1279), China officially established the Satin Academy and the Embroidery Academy, where a great number of weaving and embroidery professionals gathered together to promote the standards of silk weaving and embroidery. Dong Qichang (1555-1636), a famous Ming-dynasty (1368-1644) painter commented, "Song-dynasty embroidery boasts fine close stitches, done with one or two types of silk thread and hair-thin needles. Colors are deftly and intriguingly applied, making the whole piece splendid to look at. The embroidered mountains, rivers, pagodas, figures, birds, and flowers are all vividly brought out." He was said to have sighed in admiration, "The ten fingers must be like the spring breeze, producing such vivid pictures!"

China has four most famous types of embroidery – respectively from Suzhou, Guangdong, Hunan, and Sichuan – each with its own style and different themes. Historically, Suzhou embroidery was famous for its cats, Hunan embroidery for its tigers, Guangdong embroidery for its birds (the most famous being *One Hundred Birds Worship the Phoenix*), and Sichuan embroidery for its landscapes and human figures.

Among the four styles, Suzhou embroidery has enjoyed the greatest reputation. In the early 20th century, *Portrait of an Italian Queen* by the celebrated Suzhou embroiderer Shen Yunzhi (birth and death dates unknown) was presented to Italy as a state gift.

Suzhou embroidery is produced mainly in the Suzhou area, in addition to Yangzhou, Wuxi and Changzhou. Suzhou is abundant in silk, and people here and in the surrounding areas are known for their meticulous work style. For these two reasons, embroidery has developed quickly, with Suzhou embroidery gaining the reputation of "using needles to draw pictures with superb craft surpassing nature." Over a period of nearly 1,000 years, a great number of Suzhou people have gone into embroidery and almost every girl grows up to be a capable embroiderer, hence the local saying "Every house raises silkworms, every home does embroidery." It is said that a skillful embroiderer uses silk thread of more than 20 colors for a cat's eyes, so as to achieve the effect of brightness and vitality.

Shadow Play: the Art of Light and Shadow

In the latter half of the 18th century, a form of drama arose in France called "French Light and Shadow," which caused a great sensation when it was staged in Paris and Marseilles. This was an artistic form created on the basis of the Chinese shadow play, introduced into France by missionaries. Interestingly, for the 2004 China-France Year of Culture, Chinese artists introduced to France a new shadow play — *The Dance of Shadows*. It would be apt to say that the art of shadow play has been a witness and bridge to cultural exchange between the two countries.

The shadow play is an indigenous form of drama in China. In the 13th century it was introduced into West Asia, and by the 18th century it had spread to other parts of the world. Famed German poet Goethe (1749-1832) praised it, and the great 20th-century artist Charlie Chaplin (1889-1977) was inspired by it when he made his legendary silent films.

Shadow play: The Cow Boy and the Weaving Girl

The shadow play is in fact the world's earliest "movie art" with the accompaniment of human voice. It first appeared more than 2,000 years ago, and by the Song Dynasty this art had become highly developed with its main artistic form already established. At the time, traditional Chinese drama had not yet developed, but shadow play could already reproduce the entire lengthy story of the Three Kingdoms. It was performed in many cities and became important entertainment at festivals. During the Ming Dynasty, in the city of Beijing alone, there were dozens of shadow play troupes. It is still popular today, and its historical success has given enlightenment to the development of the modern movie.

The making of shadow-play puppets requires choice materials and skills. First, donkey hide has to be found to make the heads, limbs and torsos of the human figures, which are then painted and connected into full puppets using thread and links. During the performance, light shines on the human figures, whose silhouettes are reflected on a screen. Through their movements, they vividly act out stories, creating a world of imagination mixed with reality, which delights both the eyes and hearts of the audience.

The appeal of shadow play lies not only in its puppet-making but more in its performance. Several performers stand behind a white screen, operating puppets of different appearances, while relating the story or singing to the accompaniment of percussions or stringed musical instruments. Shadow plays from Huaxian County of Shaanxi Province are the best known, with local people even giving it another descriptive name as a "Five-person Event," because five performers are involved in each performance. The *qiansheng* is responsible for singing the different roles of a play; the *qianshou* operates the movements of the puppets; the *zuocao* is responsible for beating the gongs, bowls and percussions; the *shangdang* for playing the two-stringed fiddle and trumpet; and the *xiadang* for playing the *banhu* fiddle and trombone, as well as assisting the *qianshou*. These five people keep busy doing their particular work offstage to put on the performance.

How good a shadow play is depends on the singing and the handling of the puppets. It is no simple matter at all to operate the puppets using five bamboo sticks. It needs deft fingers on the performers' part, and a good puppeteer can dazzle the audience with the intriguing movements of the puppets.

Folk Customs

The clothing, food, housing, transportation, as well as the folk customs of the Chinese people, all reflect their inner peace, optimism, open-mindedness, and aesthetic tastes. A visitor from afar would be able to perceive all this in the hustle and bustle of the capital Bianliang of the Northern Song Dynasty (960-1127), as depicted in the famous painting *A Riverside Scene at Qingming Festival*. They could also find all this in many aspects of traditional life: the busy Tianqiao area in Beijing, the hawking of peddlers in alleys, pigeons soaring across blue skies, the leisurely life of taverns, the openness, fashion and vitality of modern Shanghai, the ambience exquisitely created in teahouses and bars, shadow boxing, and a game of go. Chinese people have long pursued soulful contentment in the midst of secular lives, trying each and every method to add meaning and joy to everyday life.

22. Urban Customs in A Riverside Scene at Qingming Festival

A Riverside Scene at Qingming Festival was a painting created by the court artist Zhang Zeduan (birth and death dates unknown), at the end of the Northern Song Dynasty (960-1127). It is now housed in the Palace Museum in Beijing.

Over the nearly 900 years since its creation, this masterpiece has generated many reproductions. Today there are over 30 reproductions collected in famous museums around the world. One copy even passed before the critical eyes of Qing Emperor Qianlong (r. 1736-1795), an art enthusiast who had believed it to be the original. That replica is now housed in the Taipei Palace Museum. In a sense, the wide range of imitations only proves the value of this precious artistic masterpiece.

What is the painting actually like then? Let us take a closer look.

A Horizontal Scroll of the Scenery along the Bianhe River

A Riverside Scene at Qingming Festival is a horizontal scroll more than five meters long. When it is unrolled from right to left, it is like opening a sluice-gate to the river of history, with the prosperous scenery of Bianliang, the capital of the Northern Song Dynasty, unveiling itself before the viewer.

The painting depicts the hustle and bustle along the banks of the Bianhe River during the Qingming Festival. By this season, the snow and ice have gone, and the cold of early spring has bidden farewell, and people are welcoming the most important festival of spring – the Qingming (Pure and Brightness) Festival, one of the 24 solar terms and a day for remembrance. On this day, people make offerings to their ancestors, a custom still observed to this day. Qingming Festival is also a day to celebrate the arrival of spring, when the lovely warm sun and the gentle breezes turn the grass intoxicatingly green. The painting starts from the right with a depiction of spring in the outskirts of the city of Bianliang: brooks gurgling in the wilderness, with cottages tucked away among trees and roads crisscrossing into the far distance. Old trees greet the breeze, their branches and twigs already tinged with light green. In the distance are boundless

fields enveloped in hazy mist. Suddenly, a group of people appear, leading several donkeys, on their way to the city. To the left, there are lines of travelers, who are either on their way to graves to make offerings or are sightseers just back from the city. Donkeys and horses are seen neighing, and people talking and laughing.

As the scroll unrolls, we come to the second section of detailed features. The Bianhe River begins to come into view. It is a river connecting south and north, on which boats busily come and go, effectively reflecting the prosperity of the time. At the start, there are only a couple of boats moored along the bank, but as the river flows leftward, it becomes wider, the water becomes swifter, and many boats are seen sailing quickly in both directions.

The scroll unveils further to the main scene in the second section, and also the focal point of the whole painting. This depicts a scene in the center of Bianliang – the Rainbow Bridge area. A magnificent-looking wooden bridge arches over the Bianhe River, with people coming and going: merchants, travelers and sightseers. Many are holding onto the railings of the bridge, looking down at the river. Some are making animated gestures, appearing to

Scene in the outskirts, in A Riverside Scene at Qingming Festival

be speaking, or shouting in surprise, while others appear astounded in fright. Underneath, a big boat is trying to pass under the bridge, its bow lower than its stern. On the bow stands a man, frantically waving his arms, his mouth wide open as if giving orders; someone is trying to correct the direction of the boat by propping his pole against the base of the bridge; some boatmen are trying hard to work on the oars, while others standing on the awning quickly bring down the sail. The boat is going forward, leaving whirls in its wake. At that critical moment as the boat has yet to pass, people on and under the bridge are all intensely absorbed in this singular event, with the rapid, whirling currents adding further tension to the scene of onlookers and boatmen.

The third section of the painting features street scenes. The Bianhe River makes a bend here and flows toward the east. Along the banks, a wide road leads to the high city gate, at the foot of which people are either resting, talking or simply looking around. Camels are passing the city gate, with only their heads seen out of the gate – all presenting a busy road scene. Past the city gate is Bianliang, a city of crisscrossing streets, with shops, teahouses, taverns, go clubs, martial arts arenas, temples, and everything imaginable, lining both sides of the streets. There is heavy traffic on the streets: carts coming and going; some people in twos or threes, either walking in a hurry or stopping for a look of whatever interests them; others in groups talking in high spirits, or looking around enjoying the street scene. Shop owners are hospitably soliciting customers. Suddenly, a cart drawn by four mules is seen rushing along, adding a sense of surprise to the leisurely scene. Here, vendors, *yamen* runners, scholars, monks, old men, and young children, all look vivid and lifelike, and all wear different facial expressions.

The three sections of this scroll painting depict different scenes of the countryside, the river, and then the urban area, each focusing on one scene: sweeping willows in the first, the Rainbow Bridge in the second, and the city gate for the third. By centering on a major scene, the picture looks quite orderly,

Scene outside the city gate, in A Riverside Scene at Qingming Festival

although many miscellaneous details have been included. The atmosphere conveyed by each of the three sections is different. The first presents a carefree atmosphere of calm and detachment; the second, tension and stimulation as enhanced by the whirling water; and the third, boundlessness and richness conveyed through trivialities and details.

The three-section tableau of the painting is presented in a rhythmic yet contrastive way. The remoteness in the beginning poses a sharp contrast to the tension at the Rainbow Bridge and the lively street scenes. In the arrangement of the scenery, there are high and low points. After a slow beginning in the first section, the picture proceeds to its climatic scene at the Rainbow Bridge, and after portraying the street scenes inside and outside the city gate in the third section, the street scenes suddenly stop. The effect of lasting appeal that Chinese fine arts emphasizes is well embodied and realized in this painting.

Urban Civilization of the Northern Song Dynasty

Urban civilization was already developed in the Tang Dynasty (618-907), with Chang'an, the capital (today's Xi'an, Shaanxi Province), as the largest city in the world at the time. There were other large cities, such as Luoyang to the east of Chang'an and Yangzhou, a commercial center in the south. Each of these cities had a population of around one million. Chang'an, in its prime, had a population that reached over 1.5 million.

By the Northern Song Dynasty, urban culture had further developed. The capital Bianliang, with a population of one million, was then the world's largest city. Although it was smaller than Tang Dynasty's Chang'an, Bianliang was commercially more prosperous. In the Five Dynasties (907-960) the city of Luoyang had started to see shops set up along its streets, and by the Northern Song Dynasty this had become the vogue, with Bianliang having more shops

Scene in front of the city gate, in A Riverside Scene at Qingming Festival

than any other city. In the cities of Chang'an and Luoyang, shops were set up in designated areas called "shopping markets," but in Bianliang there was no such restriction and shops were allowed to set up anywhere on the streets, along the riverbanks, and basically wherever there were people. The large number of shops enriched the life in the city.

Records of the Prosperity of the Capital (Dongjing menghua lu), by Meng Yuanlao (birth and death dates unknown) of the Northern Song Dynasty, describes the affluence of Bianliang. The book made note of 72 restaurants, with numerous branches and other small taverns scattered throughout the city. Commercial activities were very dynamic. One famous market, the temple fair around Daxiangguo Temple, was open five days a month, with animals, vegetables, daily necessities, embroidery, books, antiques, spices, and medical herbs all available. Meng Yuanlao called it the "Ten Thousand Families Fair," a name evoking brisk scenes in the imagination. In each district of the capital, there were entertainment areas incorporating businesses, trades and theaters, some large enough to hold audiences of thousands. The nightlife in Bianliang was rich and diverse, with restaurants, theaters and shops opened all through the night, when the city was lit as brightly as if it were day.

A Riverside Scene at Qingming Festival provides a detailed illustration of life in the capital of the Northern Song Dynasty at its prime. The highly developed urban civilization gave creative inspiration to court artist Zhang Zeduan. He chose to paint the sunny morning of a festival day, when everything seemed spirited and full of vitality – the green grass, the flowing water and the crowds of people on the streets. With meticulous brushwork, the artist endowed the city with a strong sense of action and rhythm. The painting is capable of arousing soul-stirring emotions in the viewers who, like the painter himself, would love to immerse themselves in the warm, joyous, avid, and intoxicating atmosphere.

23. Customs and Charms of Old Beijing

Mention Old Beijing and people may instantly envision caravans of camels at the foot of the Front Gate, the crowded and noisy Tianqiao area, alleys filled with hawkers' cries, life in the courtyards, an assortment of snacks such as jellied tofu and fermented soybean milk, crosstalk comedians, Beijing musical storytelling accompanied by a small drum or a single-stringed instrument – all images piecing together an ancient song echoing far into the mists of time.

Food in Old Beijing

What is most unforgettable about Old Beijing, people say, is its food, a culture most commonplace and most closely related to people, with most distinctive local flavors.

Quanjude Roast Duck Restaurant, the most famous restaurant in Beijing, was founded by Yang Quanren (birth and death dates unknown) in 1866 – the fifth year of Emperor Tongzhi's reign (r. 1862-1874). Yang invited a celebrated cook who had once worked for the Qing (1616-1911) court kitchen, and together they created the roast duck, prepared by hanging it in an oven. A full-duck banquet consists of cold and hot dishes, in addition to soup, all prepared with duck.

Donglaishun is a Muslim restaurant renowned for its hotpot mutton. Its founder was Ding Deshan (birth and death dates unknown). The mutton here is all choice cuts carefully prepared with all types of spices. Besides hotpot mutton, the restaurant also serves pies with minced mutton, rice porridge and dumplings – all popular with customers from all walks of life.

Shaguoju is a restaurant first set up in 1741, the sixth year of Emperor Qianlong's reign (r. 1736-1795). It is famous for three specialties: deep-fried dishes of pig liver or deer tail, stewed pig's head, and slices of meat prepared simply with water. Slices of meat can be served either with soy sauce, sesame oil, minced garlic, hot and spicy oil, or by cooking it together with cabbage, vermicelli, dried shrimps, mushrooms, and broth in a hotpot. Other famous dishes include three-white hotpot, meatball hotpot, braised preserved cabbage, etc.

Barbecue Ji was founded by Ji Decai (birth and death dates unknown) in 1848, the 28th year of Qing Emperor Daoguang's reign (r. 1821-1850), serving barbecue mutton, using date, pine and cypress wood as fuel. Over smoke and fire, diners hold either a cup of alcohol or a sesame-seed cake in one hand and a pair of chopsticks about 33 centimeters long in the other. They pick up the mutton, which has been marinating in a mixture of different types of spices, and put it on the iron grill, eating as they cook it themselves. Another barbecue restaurant is called Barbecue Yuan, which serves veal instead of mutton.

The Fangshan Restaurant was first opened in 1925 by Zhao Renzhai (birth and death dates unknown), a former servant of the Qing court. The restaurant is located on the northern shore of Beihai in Beijing. The dishes are prepared according to recipes used by the Qing court, with particular attention paid to the color, aroma, taste, and form. There are nearly 100 famous dishes, including stewed abalone, stewed venison, stir-fried chicken, arhat shrimp, etc. The restaurant also serves snacks like pea-flour cakes, kidney-bean-flour rolls, small corn-flour buns, cakes with meat fillings, all looking cute and appealing.

There is an "official cuisine" restaurant in Beijing – the Tan Family Cuisine. Tan Zongjun (1846-1888), the restaurant's founder, was a member of the Imperial Academy of the Qing Dynasty. The Tan Family Cuisine falls under Guangdong cuisine, with seafood such as abalone and sea cucumber as the main features. The restaurant is furnished with rosewood furniture and paintings by famous artists.

Food culture in Old Beijing has helped to create an earthly living world of lasting appeal. Xiao Qian (1910-1999), a famous contemporary writer, recalled the snacks of Beijing: "When I recall the years I drifted from place to place, what did I miss most about Beijing? It is fermented soybean milk, buckwheat cakes, 'donkey' rolls, seasoned millet flour mush prepared with hot water poured out of a big-bellied copper kettle, and hot, deep-fried sausages." Many intellectuals moving to Taiwan from Beijing always felt homesick and nostalgic, missing the foods and snacks of Beijing, such as Quanjude roast duck, barbecue mutton, mutton hotpot, pea-flour cakes, and frozen pears hawked on cold winter nights.

Alleys and Hawkers' Cries

The glamour of Old Beijing comes not only from the magnificent city gate towers, but also from those narrow alleys, or *hutong*, as they are called in the Beijing dialect.

The alleys in Beijing first appeared in the Yuan Dynasty (1206-1368), as mentioned in the drama, *Scholar Zhang Boils the Sea*, in which a maid says, "You can come look for me in Zhuantar Hutong…" This shows that Zhuantar Alley, west of South Xisi Street, already existed back in the Yuan Dynasty.

Alleys in Old Beijing had their own special flavor, and their names alone were perhaps poetic enough to give flight to people's imagination (e.g., Apricot Flower Day, Flower Twig and Moonlight), or practical enough to reflect the lifestyle of ordinary people (e.g., Tea Leaf Alley, Alcohol Alley and Eggplant Alley, to name just a few). More interestingly, according to the recollections of elders, different alleys had different smells. For example, Money and Grain Alley smelled of cabbage, Hat Alley of sugar-coated haws on sticks, and Sedan-chair Alley of fermented soy milk.

Alleys in Old Beijing also echoed with the cries of vendors hawking their wares and the sounds of particular percussion instruments. High and low, distant and near, the cries had a rhythmic, lasting appeal, such as cries in the early morning to sell deep-fried dough-sticks and sesame-seed cakes, evening cries for selling fruit, and midnight cries for noodles, steamed buns and wonton soup. Some vendors did not call out their goods, but used percussion instruments to solicit customers. Once people heard metallic clicking sounds, they knew the barber

Gate pier

was coming; or with the sound of gongs, they knew a circus was staging a performance. The sound of wooden clappers signaled the coming of an oil vendor, while the noise of a drum-shaped rattle meant the arrival of a peddler selling daily necessities.

Particular attention was paid to the tones and styles of alley cries to attract customers. The cries had to be vital, the voice crisp, the words clearly articulated, and the tone melodious with floral embellishment and smoothness, as well as a dragging tune, especially on the last word. The cries using the Beijing dialect were hence rich with a local flavor. Besides being musical, the cries of vendors possessed literary charm, with rhyming and exaggerated modes employed to express joy or humor. For example, a watermelon vendor hawked: "Come have a bite, of this ice-cold, crisp fruit, a moon-shaped slice, as big as a boat, pulp as sweet as a Mid-autumn moon-cake, palm leaves fail to shoo away bees taking it for a hive; sweeten your mouth for just a penny!" Such cries brimmed with the joy and humor of ordinary people.

Bustling Tianqiao

The Tianqiao area in Old Beijing was a place famous for spotlighting Beijing's folk customs, with theaters specializing in different types of folk performances, amusement playgrounds, taverns, teahouses, food stands, and kiosks selling daily necessities. Peking Opera, Heibei Bangzi, Pingxi Opera, puppet shows, shadow plays, comic talk, acrobatics, magic performances, and other diverse performing arts all gathered here, alongside more than 100 snacks, including jellied tofu, seasoned flour mush, deep-fried tofu, cakes, to name just a few. A galaxy of shops sold miscellaneous goods and such daily necessities as clothing, furniture, secondhand shoes and books, curios, etc. There were also dental clinics, drugstores, fortunetellers, barbers, and vendors of all kinds. It was a clamorous place full of noise and excitement.

Among the entertainers of Tianqiao, the majority were engaged in acrobatics and *quyi* (Chinese folk vocal art forms rich in local flavor, including

Colors of autumn
in Beijing

balladeering, storytelling, comic talk, clapper talk, crosstalk, etc.), alongside those in local operas, circuses and martial arts. Among them were three groups of entertainers with unique appearance, speech and behavior, and most of all, superb performing skills. They were called the "eight eccentrics," engaging in comic talk, vocal mimicry, balladeering, and *qigong*. One of them, named "Jester King," could break a 20cm-thick stone with his palm, or cut it into two with his index, middle and ring fingers. The performance of the "eight eccentrics" truly drew the admiration of audiences.

In addition to the "eight eccentrics," other entertainers also boasted superb skills and gained high repute among audiences. "Everybody Happy," a vocal impersonator, used a fan to cover his face while imitating the tones and voices of different people. His most popular performance was called "Five Kids Making Trouble at School." At the beginning of the performance, the audience could hear the snoring of people sound asleep, followed by a cock crowing at dawn, a woman waking up her husband, breastfeeding an infant, the elder son getting up to pee, the husband yawning, going to the mill to pull the donkey out, door opening and closing, thudding of the donkey's hooves on the ground, bells clanking, the woman urging her son to go to school, the elder son asking for money to buy steamed buns for breakfast and singing on his way to school, readings by children at school, whispers, laughter, wails and bickering after the teacher leaves the classroom, scolding – all sounds cleverly reproduced and remarkably true to life.

Most visitors to Tianqiao were ordinary people. The boisterous scenes, noisy crowds, colorful streamers, and delicious snacks, all brought everyone contentment, joy, and more importantly, spiritual consolation.

Temple Fairs in Old Beijing

Temple fairs in Old Beijing were regularly held around large and well-known temples, which had their particular flavors and styles. Visiting temple fairs was a major pastime in the lives of Beijing residents. According to 1930 statistics, there were 20 temples, 16 in the suburbs and two in downtown area. The most famous temple fairs were the White Pagoda Temple Fair, Huguo Temple Fair, Longfu Temple Fair, Yonghe Lamasery Fair, Baiyun Temple Fair, Pantao Temple Fair, and Changdian Fair.

The Longfu Temple Fair was the largest of its kind in the city. Weng Ouhong (1908-1994), a playwright and a frequent visitor to the fair, recorded a detailed description of the spectacular event:

"The Longfu Temple Fair starts right outside the streets that lead to the gate of the temple. Along them gather all sorts of stands and stores, selling second-hand goods, rare birds, dogs and cats of rare breeds, books (age-old books not commonly seen outside the fair), and tea. Inside the temple, there are three streets. Down the middle street, there are stalls selling daily necessities and snacks, as well as arenas for entertainment, such as flagpole waving, comic duets (folk art with one doing pantomime as the other hides behind him doing all the speaking or singing), and *pingshu* (folk art with the performer telling a long story using a folding fan, a handkerchief and a gavel as props). Down the western street are stands selling goldfish, shuttlecocks, spare parts of musical instruments, and Peking Opera scripts. Along the eastern street are stalls selling different figurines made from materials diverse as leather, flour dough and wood. Among them, the silhouette portraits of famous Peking Opera actors are made absolutely lifelike."

Temple fairs were entertainment venues for ordinary people, therefore, everything in them was closely related to daily life. Yet temple fairs also stood out beyond everyday life, thus giving both physical and spiritual pleasure to visitors, be they male or female, young or old.

Leisure Life in Old Beijing

The leisure lives of people in Old Beijing were refined, balanced and carefree, brimming with the charm of the ancient capital.

Leisure life in Beijing may be well described in one phrase: "having fun," or in the words of Beijingers, "looking for fun." Chen Jiangong (b. 1949), a contemporary Chinese writer, once commented, "Beijingers like to have fun, and are good at looking for fun." To raise a bird is fun, to fly a kite is fun, to sip wine with a piece of garlic is fun, and to sing an aria of Peking Opera or listen to it is also great fun. Yet the most common way of enjoying a leisurely life for ordinary Beijingers is to drink tea and wine.

There were a great number of teahouses in Old Beijing, and people from all walks of life would meet for tea – reporters, writers, actors, chess players, teachers, students, and craftspeople (the latter usually coming to snag customers). People would stop to rest at a teahouse on their way to exercise their pet birds. They would either hang the cages on a pole or put them on the table, sipping tea while enjoying the creatures. Thus, various kinds of birds would be chirping together. A teahouse was a public place for socializing, as well as a compact society where comedies and tragedies of everyday life transpired. Lao She (1899-1966), a famous Chinese playwright, made superb vivid descriptions of happenings in a teahouse, in his play *Teahouse (Chaguan)*, a classic work in the history of Chinese literature.

A large number of restaurants were scattered throughout the city of Old Beijing, but most of the large ones were located in business areas, while small taverns were set up at the entrance to alleys. These taverns usually had simple dishes to go with wine, such as boiled peanuts, dried tofu, preserved eggs, smoked fish,

White pigeons over the roof of an old house in Beijing

and fried shrimps. Inside the taverns, there were usually several big vats, their mouths covered with big lids painted red, which served as tables, hence these taverns were nicknamed "Big Wine Vats."

Besides drinking tea and wine, Beijingers had other ways to enjoy life, such as raising goldfish and pigeons, flying kites, raising crickets and grasshoppers, collecting porcelain ware, facial masks, potted plants, clay and dough figurines… They could find pleasure in all types of trivial things, to make their lives more interesting and joyful.

Beijingers liked to raise goldfish, a hobby developed as early as the Jin (1115-1234) and Yuan (1206-1368) dynasties. They enjoyed setting up goldfish tanks, which, together with persimmon trees, became an indispensable decoration for a traditional courtyard known as *siheyuan*.

Beijingers also liked to raise pigeons, with pleasure derived from releasing the birds to fly. Some people liked to tie pigeon whistles to the birds' tail feathers. Wang Shixiang (b. 1914), a folklorist, remarked that the sound of pigeon whistles had become a symbol of Beijing. He said, "In Beijing, be it in warm spring or high summer, clear autumn or icy cold winter, whistling sounds can be heard in the sky. Thick at one moment, thin at another, remote or near, high or low, quick or slow, at all times they hover and echo, like refreshing music from heaven." He added, "This appealing sound wakes people up from their dreams, draws their eyes up into the distant firmament, and brings joy to children and adults alike, for who knows how many times."

Following the changes of the times, the lifestyle of Beijing people has also changed. At the end of the 20th century and the beginning of the 21st century, there appeared Bar Street in Sanlitun, Guijie Street in Dongzhimen, and another Bar Street around Shichahai Lake, for people to enjoy themselves in their spare time. Shichahai Lake used to be a deserted place, but it suddenly became "attractive" at the beginning of the new century. A variety of bars now stand shoulder by shoulder, with interesting names such as Blue Lotus, Listening to the Moon and Hello Bar. These catchy names, if threaded together, could make for an amazing poem, from which people would be able to feel the folk flavor of the Shichahai Lake district, now better known by foreign visitors as Houhai, with the glamorous charm of 21st-century Beijing.

Beijing is a city that belongs to yesterday, today and tomorrow, one scholar says, and this is true.

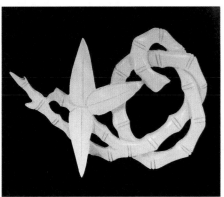

24. Modern Glamour of Old Shanghai

Old Shanghai was the most internationalized metropolis in the modern history of China. *All about Shanghai*, an English book published in Shanghai in 1935, thus introduced the city to Westerners: Shanghai was the sixth largest city in the world, the Paris of the East, and perhaps the most cosmopolitan city on Earth.

In the minds of the Chinese people at the time, Shanghai was a "modern" city, a perceptual acknowledgment of the metropolitan culture of Old Shanghai. "Modernity" is an integral part of the city, an open, fashionable and dynamic place full of the charm of the time.

The Most Open City

As an open, international city, Old Shanghai was the earliest and quickest to draw ideas from the modern West. Someone once pointed out that Shanghai, situated along the Bund geographically, had no concept of boundaries or demarcations, and that perhaps constituted one reason for its openness.

According to historical records, a variety of modern urban facilities were brought to Shanghai from the West in the mid-19th century: banks were introduced to China in 1848, European-style streets in 1856, gas lamps in 1865, telephones in 1881, running water in 1884, automobiles in 1901, and trolley buses in 1908. The Lumiere brothers of France invented film in 1895, and eight months later a film theater turned up on Zhapu Road in Hongkou District in Shanghai. By the 1930s, Shanghai had kept pace with the most developed cities in the world in terms of applied modern facilities.

A characteristic of Old Shanghai as a metropolis was its opening to the outside world, as the largest gateway through which Western culture found its way into China. From the period 1840-1949, besides those innovations mentioned above, other different types of culture, both material and intellectual, were introduced to Shanghai, including newspapers, music, paintings, stage plays, dancing, circuses, magic shows, gramophones, cameras, telegraphs, electric fans, sewing machines, sprinklers, business suits, coffee, food, beer, the Gregorian calendar, the weekly system, Western-style wedding ceremonies, libraries, museums, the police system, and the practice of boards of directors for companies. All these phenomena then gradually spread inland into the rest of China. Western academic classics, translated by Yan Fu (1854-1921), and Western novels, by Lin Shu (1852-1924), were also first published in Shanghai.

Old Shanghai's cosmopolitan openness was best reflected in the buildings along the Bund. There were 28 buildings of ten or more stories, representing 17 classical architectural styles of Europe, including English, Russian, German and Austrian, hence its moniker as a "World Architectural Fair." For example, Sassoon House at No. 20 Bund (today's northern building of the Peace Hotel) is a 13-story building, its rooms extravagantly furnished in the style of different countries, including China, Britain, France, Germany, India, Japan, Italy, and Spain. It was therefore acclaimed as the "No. 1 House in the Far East." Another example is the Great Britain Club (later the Shanghai Club, and today's Dongfeng Restaurant), located at No. 2 Bund. It is known for its Western Restaurant, which was an over 300-square-meter space without a single pillar. Its bar was 36

Calendar picture from Shanghai in the early 20th century

meters deep, claiming the title of the "longest bar in the Far East." Still another example is the Building of the Hongkong and Shanghai Banking Corporation (today used by the Shanghai Pudong Development Bank). The building was constructed following the Greek style, with ionic pillars and two bronze lions at the gate transported from Britain. The pillars in the lobby, the wainscot and the grounds were all furnished with costly European marble. The upper walls and the dome of the lobby were covered with 200 square meters of colorful murals, all designed by British artists and rendered in mosaic by Italian craftsmen. This building hence was acclaimed as "the most extravagant architecture in the Far East, from the Suez Canal to the Bering Strait."

As the most open city in China, Shanghai was home to the largest number of international residents in China. In 1942, the foreign population exceeded 150,000, from 58 countries including Britain, the US, France, Germany, Russia,

India, and Japan. Among them were rich and poor people. For some who could not make a living at home, Shanghai was a city that was able to help them realize their dreams. "Shanghai-bound!" was a classic adventure.

As an international metropolis, Shanghai once attracted many literary celebrities who gave lectures here, such as US philosopher John Dewey (1859-1952), British philosopher Bertrand Russell (1872-1970), great physicist Albert Einstein (1879-1955), Indian poet Rabindranath Tagore (1861-1941), and US film artist Charlie Chaplin (1889-1977). These men brought to Shanghai the latest ideas in the fields of world culture and arts.

Shanghai's openness was also seen in a historic episode of taking in more than 30,000 Jews who took refuge there during World War II. This number was larger than the combined totals of European Jews who found asylum in Canada, Australia, India, South Africa, and New Zealand. Jewish people escaping the clutches of the Nazis came to Shanghai because there was no demand for a visa or other documents to enter the city. Shanghai became an ark for Jewish refugees fleeing the hell of Europe, and they lived there until the end of World War II.

Visitors to Shanghai, no matter which country they come from, always feel the warmth and ease of finding a home rather than just a hotel. An Englishman wrote on the eve of the Japanese attacks on Shanghai in 1937, "To most of us, Shanghai is our permanent home." This well demonstrates that Shanghai has been an international metropolis not only in the sense of material and technological prosperity but also in the deeper sense of inner cultural outlook.

Fashion Seekers

Old Shanghai people were keen on fashion, a typical cosmopolitan perception of the city. This perception reflects not only the habits and customs of Shanghai people but also their spirit and culture.

In Old Shanghai, people's pursuit of fashion mainly referred to their pursuit of Western lifestyles, in which cafés and dancing were foremost. Cafés were very popular with Old Shanghai people, the most famous of which were Xinya and Sullivan on Nanjing Road, Constantine and Balkan at the Jing'an Temple intersection, and Little Men opposite the Cathay Theater. It was the fashion of the day for literati in Shanghai to come to these cafés at dusk each day to enjoy rich, fragrant coffee, while having discussions with friends. It is no exaggeration to say that literary circles in Shanghai in the 1920s and 1930s were immersed in the aromatic ambience of cafés.

Old Shanghai also boasted a large number of ballrooms. In 1946, about 3,300 professional dancing girls were registered with the government. Old Shanghai was acclaimed as "the city without night in the East," which shows how rich Shanghai nightlife was, with ballrooms playing an important role. Famous ballrooms included the Paramount, Metropolitan Garden, the Lido, and St. Anna, to name just a few. The Paramount orchestra was formed by Russian musicians, who played the latest US jazz. This ballroom is still well known to people today, because contemporary writer Bai Xianyong (b. 1937) mentions it in two of his stories, "The Last Night of Miss Jin" and "Everlasting Yin Xueyan."

Old Shanghai people pursued fashion and Western style, yet it did not mean that they were westernized in all aspects. In habits and customs of everyday life, Old Shanghai people always preserved their own native culture, that is, the features and temperament of Jiangsu-Zhejiang culture.

Let us take food for example. There were many Western restaurants in Old Shanghai, of which Yipinxiang was famed for its extravagant furnishings – including a caged leopard for the enjoyment of diners. Zeng Pu (1872-1935), author of the novel *Flowers of the Sea of Retribution (Niehaihua)*, at the end of the Qing Dynasty (1616-1911), described the scene of experiencing Western cuisine in Yipinxiang. Many wealthy people in Shanghai were keen on eating Western food, and people with less means would also take their families out to try it on festive occasions. Trying Western food was in vogue, popularly known as "having a big dish" or "having a big dinner." People from outside Shanghai would also take the experience of eating Western food as an indispensable activity of experiencing Shanghai lifestyle when visiting the city.

However, eating Western food has never become a mainstay, but been treated as an embellishment to Shanghai people's cuisine and beverages, and despite all the years, their cooking culture has preserved local and regional traditions and flavors.

From ancient times, Shanghai has been an area where the main crop is rice, the staple food for Shanghai people who eat it for three meals a day. The main staple food provided by local restaurants is also rice. Sometimes vegetables, salted meat, sausages or pork are added to make flavored rice of various kinds. Homemade Shanghai dishes use simple ingredients like pork, chicken, duck, egg, dried bamboo shoots, green beans, tofu, and mushrooms, with the best-known dishes being dried bamboo shoots with stewed meat, shredded meat with green beans, and deep-fried tofu with stewed meat. They are delicious yet economic. Snacks in Shanghai are also tasty, such as Nanxiang steamed buns with minced meat stuffing, Ningbo sweet dumplings, noodles with chopped green onions, etc. These snacks are carefully prepared, delicious yet cheap, and typical of cuisine south of the Yangtze River.

Shikumen and the Customs of the Alleys

Shikumen is a type of residential architecture that came into being with the urbanization of Shanghai. Over the years, these buildings have served as the major accommodation for most Shanghai residents.

Shikumen architecture was first introduced into Shanghai in the 1850s and 1860s. This was a type of building that used less land, smaller quantities of building materials and less money. It usually consisted of three rooms upstairs and three rooms downstairs. The middle room downstairs served as a living

room, and the same layout was applied upstairs. Smaller-scale Shikumen buildings were later constructed, with two rooms upstairs and two rooms downstairs; or even smaller: with one room upstairs and one room downstairs. The door of a Shikumen building was made of thick black wood framed with slates of granite or red stone from Ningbo, Zhejiang Province, hence the name "Shikumen," or literally Stone Warehouse Gate. Later, to cater to the needs of the rich middle class, new – style Shikumen housing appeared: the high walls and black gates were removed; bathrooms and gas stoves equipped; and the small yard turned into a garden – known to people as Renovated Shikumen.

Owing to high rents, a Shikumen building usually housed about six or seven families, and sometimes, incredibly, more than a dozen. The residents usually came from different places across China, to engage in a variety of occupations, and with different lifestyles and interests, but all lived under the same roof, thus forming unique scenes of interest. *Under the Roof of Shanghai*, a classic play written by contemporary playwright Xia Yan (1900-1995), vividly describes the tragicomedy of a group of ordinary people living in a Shikumen building in east Shanghai in the 1930s.

On the second floor of a Shikumen building, there was a room called "pavilion" or more exactly garret. It was usually situated above the kitchen, about ten square meters in size. The garret, being denied access to the sun all year round, was cold in winter and hot in summer. The rent for it was cheap, usually four silver dollars a month. The renters varied from office clerks to industrial workers, shop apprentices, college students, senior-high-school students, freelancers, artists, playwrights, and musicians. Sometimes, a few writers shared one such garret. In the 1920s, many well-known writers like Lu Xun (1881-1936), Mao Dun (1896-1981) and Ba Jin (1904-2005), and artists like Xu Beihong (1895-1953) and Liu Haisu (1896-1994), once lived and worked in the Shikumen buildings, and some of them even in garrets.

Shikumen buildings standing side by side then formed alleys, or *lilong* or *longtang* in Shanghai dialect. The width of the alleys ranged from the widest of four meters to the narrowest of less than three meters. The alleys witnessed the everyday life of ordinary Shanghai people, who ate in the alley, washed clothes in the alley, cleaned vegetables in the alley, as well as emptied their night-stools in the alley. In summer, every household put a dining table out in the alley, with the family sitting around it to have dinner. In the evening, many people would place reclining wooden chairs or bamboo couches at the entrance to the alley, and cool them off with water before sitting down and enjoying the evening breeze.

One characteristic of alley life was openness. In the alley, family life was closely related to social life, without much privacy. What a family ate, how much clothing a family had, what financial situation a family was in, or what relatives a family had, was all known to everyone living in the alley. Some people say that the open-mindedness of the Shanghai people may have derived from the lack of privacy in the alleys.

There were many small shops in alleys, and more at entrances to the alleys, including clothing shops, rice shops, the butcher's, the tailor's, and the barber's. There were also vendors who walked through the alleys to sell snacks from morning till late into the night, their cries echoing through the alleys. This is similar to Beijing. But snacks sold in the Shanghai alleys were all southern-style snacks, such as steaming wonton soup, ham *zongzi* (sticky rice wrapped in reed leaves), sweet rice porridge with lotus seeds, ice-cream, and deep-fried fermented dried tofu. When people living on a second floor heard the hawking of vendors, they would tie a rope to a bamboo basket in which they had placed a small pot and money. They would drop it

A Wonton Vendor, *cartoon by Feng Zikai (1899-1975)*

Buying Zongzi , *cartoon by Feng Zikai*

down through the window, and within minutes the vendor would put steaming wonton soup, or *zongzi*, in the pot. Vendors and residents were quite familiar with each other, and would not have to talk to know what the customers wanted.

Although ordinary Shanghai people lived in the alleys, they also maintained close relationships with the outside world and felt the influence of Western modernity – especially people from the middle class and intellectuals. Writers frequented foreign-language bookstores, where they could get the newest books from Western countries. Ye Lingfeng (1905-1975), a contemporary writer, recalled the day he saw in a bookstore *Ulysses* by James Joyce (1882-1941), published by the Shakespeare & Co. Bookshop in Paris. Excited, he paid 70 cents for this book, which was worth 10 US dollars. This story reveals how intellectuals in Shanghai were closely linked to the outside world. Although they lived in Shikumen buildings, their thoughts and tastes were deeply influenced by Western culture.

At the end of the 20th century and the beginning of the 21st century, there appeared in Shanghai a famous entertainment resort named Xintiandi, renovated from the Shikumen alleys. The paths and the exterior walls still use black bricks. However, the furnishings inside are in a modern style, and cafés, restaurants, music bars, fashion outlets, and movie theaters all congregate here. Tourists are often deeply impressed by the elegance and modernity, calm and vitality of the place. "The aged feel nostalgic, the young feel fashionable, foreign visitors feel very Chinese, and Chinese people see it as Western style," is how some people sum up the style of the resort. Others claim it as the "Fisherman's Wharf" of China. So it would be apt to say that this entertainment resort is a true demonstration of Shanghai people's genius, combining modernity and tradition to create things both original and fashionable.

Shanghai is China's most fashionable, dynamic city, a cosmopolis whose glamour lies more than anything else in its openness, its leading role in new things and trends, and its omniscient vitality.

25. Traditional Costumes

China boasts a brilliant history of clothing, some dating it to 4,000 years ago, when Chinese people invented silk. Around the 18th century, when the rococo style arose in Europe, it became a fashion for aristocrats to wear Chinese-style costumes to festive balls. In fact, as early as in the Tang Dynasty (618-907), China already led the world in its clothing industry. The clothes at the time were innovatively bright in color, light and soft in texture, flowing and graceful in style, and valuable in artistic terms, as evident in the extant Tang-style clothes preserved to this day in the Shoso-in Treasures of Japan.

Graceful Tang-style Fashion

An important moment of the APEC Summit occurs when heads of member states pose for the collective photograph of all in clothing provided by the host country – an opportunity favored by photojournalists. Each host country takes into consideration its aesthetic tastes and cultural traditions in the design of the garments. At the 2001 APEC Summit, China as the host country provided heads of state with Tang-style apparel, attracting worldwide attention for its rich and strong Chinese characteristics.

This attire is named after the Tang Dynasty, a prosperous era in Chinese history. The label "Tang-style apparel" gives recognition to ancient Chinese culture, though not necessarily meaning this design was popular in the Tang Dynasty. The name today is simply a term for a special Chinese-style design in clothing.

Tang-style fashion in reality combines the Manchu clothing style of the Qing Dynasty (1616-1911) with the style of Western suits. Such designs are available for both men and women.

Tang-style apparel has four main elements: first, it is usually front-buttoned, though most of women's costumes are buttoned on the left, a design not only displaying the characteristics of the Chinese style but looking quite graceful; second, it always has a vertical collar, which sets off the wearer's demeanor; third, it has no seams between the sleeves and the main part of the costume; fourth, it uses handmade stylish cloth buttons.

The designs, the source of the vivacity of the Tang-style apparel, present a strong national flavor. These designs, in round shapes, usually feature peony, plum, orchid, bamboo, and chrysanthemum to symbolize fortune, dignity and purity; or feature Chinese characters meaning blessing, position, longevity, or double happiness. Today, Chinese people love to wear Tang-style clothing on happy occasions or during festivals wishing for blessing and happiness.

Tang-style attire is also favored by film directors. In the TV drama, *The Oranges Are Red*, directed by Li Shaohong (b. 1955), the heroine Xiuhe shows off dozens of Tang-style costumes. This wardrobe was designed on the basis of the robes worn by princesses of the Qing Dynasty with small vertical collars. Made of quality silks and embroidered with different kinds of flowers in the Chinese style, the outfits look refined and elegant with their high aesthetics gaining public appreciation.

Beautiful Cheongsam

The cheongsam (known in China as *qipao*), which enjoyed initial popularity in the 1920s, was first designed by Shanghai people, combining the style of Manchu women's traditional gowns with the style of clothing in southern China and of European evening dresses. It is close-fitting and sleeveless, has a high neck and slit skirt, worn with matching permed hair, high-heeled shoes, nylon stockings and brooches, to fully display a woman's graceful curves, elegant carriage and dignified manner.

In the first half of the 20th century, the cheongsam, with Western-style overcoat and waistcoat to match, became the fashion for Chinese female movie stars, and numerous fans across the country followed suit.

The cheongsam is also a fashion style favored by Chinese film directors. At the beginning of the 21st century, Wang Jiawei (b. 1958), known internationally as Wang Kar-wei, directed the film *In the Mood for Love*, in which the heroine wears 26 cheongsams. These cheongsams, of graceful colors and designs, refined and elegant, have provided a chance for world audiences to appreciate the charm of Chinese women in cheongsam.

The beauty of the cheongsam is implicit and delicate, vibrant yet reserved, dignified yet natural. It takes full consideration of the characteristics of Chinese women's figures, using different kinds of materials, colors and styles, to best display their grace and dignity. The cheongsam has changed people's ideas about Chinese clothes being "conservative," and has been gaining great acclaim in the international community.

Natural Wax Printing

About 2,000 years ago, wax printing appeared in China, with batiks being found among the goods traded along the Silk Road during the Han Dynasty (206 BC-AD 220). It was also found in the relics of the Northern Dynasties (386-581) unearthed in the Xinjiang Uygur Autonomous Region. By the Tang Dynasty, wax printing techniques had matured, and scenes of batik making were reproduced in the murals of Grotto 130 of the Mogao Grottoes in Dunhuang, Gansu Province.

Wax printing has long been a widespread technique used in the history of Chinese fashion. It was applied across the country, from the northwest to the northeast, from the southwestern border areas to the lake regions south of the lower Yangtze River. Guizhou Province is where wax printing is the most widely used, and Guizhou women have a special love for batik. Today, in some parts of the province, women's clothing, headwear, aprons, and skirts are mostly made of batik. Batik is still loved by people today because of its natural, dynamic beauty.

Emperor Qianlong's Concubine Ornamenting Her Hair, *Qing Dynasty*

Commander-
in-chief's Wife
Worshipping
Buddha *(detail)*,
*Tang Dynasty,
mural in Grotto 130,
Dunhuang*

During the dyeing process, beeswax is applied to prevent some parts of the cloth from being dyed, so as to acquire a special dyeing effect. The process goes as follows: first, the beeswax is melted, and a copper knife is used to apply the melted wax to the cloth to form designs. After the beeswax has dried, the cloth is put into a vat of indigo for dyeing. Afterwards, the dyed cloth is put into water and boiled to get rid of the beeswax, before it is rinsed. This is how white designs appear against a background of blue.

Special "ice cracks" appear during the dyeing process. This is because when the beeswax dries, it develops cracks, which absorb indigo in the process of dyeing, thus forming the beautiful natural lines resembling breaking ice. These lines are naturally formed, just like the crackles on the surface of crackleware. They represent the beauty and soul of batiks.

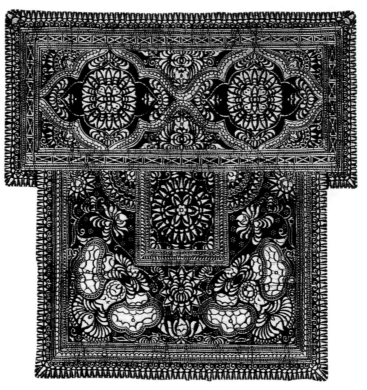

Batik of Miao people,
Guizhou Province

Splendid Stage Costumes

Stage costumes are an important part of traditional Chinese clothing. They have developed from ordinary clothes and embodied many characteristics of traditional Chinese clothing.

Stage costumes are referred to as *xingtou* in the Chinese language, and each role in a play has his or her own special costume. Audiences can usually tell the identity of a role by the stage costume. For example, young female characters are divided into two kinds, *qingyi* and *huadan*. The former are the heroines, who usually possess a virtuous and dignified character, such as Lady Mengjiang in *Lady Mengjiang Mourns Her Husband at the Great Wall* or Sun Shangxiang in

Making Sacrifices to the River. Their costumes are usually simple and elegant, typically in the black. The *huadan* are usually lively young girls, and therefore their costumes are bright and colorful. *Huadan* usually wear a coat and a skirt, with a sleeveless jacket and waist sash with ornaments. The *huadan* costume is the most beautiful of all stage costumes.

The costumes used in Chinese plays match well with the personalities, identities and moods of the roles. For example, the *qingyi* usually lead a hard life and have a melancholy character, therefore their costumes are usually in cooler colors, while the *huadan* roles are usually lively and cheerful, with the gorgeous clothing well suiting their sanguine personalities.

A Court Lady with Head Ornament *(detail), by Zhou Fang (birth and death dates unknown), Tang Dynasty*

Chinese stage costumes reflect the exquisite beauty pursued by traditional Chinese aesthetics. The image of Zhao Yun (?-229), a historical figure of the Three Kingdoms Period (220-280) and the hero in the famous Peking Opera *The Slopes of Changban,* serves as a good example. In the Changban hillside battle, Zhao Yun ventures alone into the enemy camp to rescue Liu Bei (161-223), his master. The story displays Zhao Yun's loyalty, valiance and heroic bearing. Onstage, Zhao Yun wears red facial makeup (symbolizing loyalty and heroism), a splendid robe, and a dragon-design cape, with four triangular streamers waving on his back. With his agile movements, the streamers fly, and the robe and ornaments gleam, thus vividly displaying a valiant and heroic image on the stage.

The long sleeves of the female characters in traditional Chinese stage costumes are an interesting phenomenon to observe. The sleeves, long and loose, are exercised smoothly like flowing water or flying clouds by skillful actors, hence the Chinese name Water Sleeves. Any Peking Opera actors playing female roles need to learn how to toss out and bring in the Water Sleeves – a skill not easy to master. Excellent sleeve performances, set against supple and graceful movements and the melodious singing of female characters, produce a dramatic effect, drawing audiences into the extremely sentimental world of the female characters.

26. Culinary Delights in China

Chinese cuisine is a brilliant facet of Chinese culture, which is proven by the fact that Chinese restaurants are found scattered everywhere throughout the world. Today, the culinary industry is developing even more rapidly than before. A decade ago, Beijing had a few thousand restaurants, while today there are over 100,000 restaurants of different sizes in the city.

Local Chinese Cuisines

It is widely acknowledged that from the Ming (1368-1644) and Qing (1616-1911) dynasties onwards, there arose eight schools of cuisine, respectively from Shandong, Sichuan, Guangdong, Fujian, Jiangsu, Zhejiang, Hunan, and Anhui provinces. In addition to these traditional cuisines, the culinary industry in China has undergone great changes, as almost every place has its own local specialties, just as different cuisines have gathered in one place. In big cities like Beijing, Shanghai and Guangzhou, one can taste all the familiar and famed dishes from around the country.

A glimpse of Slender West Lake in Yangzhou,
Jiangsu Province

Sichuan, known as Nature's Storehouse, is also a storehouse of cuisine. Here, each and every restaurant provides delicious yet economic culinary fare. The ingredients for Sichuan cuisine are simple but the spices used are quite different. Sichuan cuisine is famous for its spicy and hot food, yet just being hot and spicy does not necessarily distinguish it from other hot and spicy cuisines such as Hunan or Guizhou cuisine. What is really special about Sichuan cuisine is the use of Chinese prickly ash seeds, the taste of which leaves a feeling of numbness on one's tongue and mouth. Besides this unique spice, Sichuan dishes are also usually prepared with other spices like chili pepper. Using fermented bean sauce and a set of unique cooking methods, Sichuan cuisine is now famous and popular across the world. Over recent years, there have appeared many more renowned restaurants specializing in Sichuan cuisine, such as Tan Family Fish Head.

Guangdong Province is located in southern China, with a moderate climate and abundant produce all year round. As one of the earliest ports open to foreign trade, the province has developed a culinary culture with its own characteristics that has exerted a far-reaching influence on other parts of China. Guangdong cuisine is famous for its seafood as well as for its originality and refined cooking processes. Various soups in this cuisine have become loved by people all over the country.

Zhejiang cuisine is light and exquisite, as representative of food from along the lower Yangtze River. One famous dish is West Lake Vinegar Fish, which looks delicate and tastes tender, with the refreshing flavors of nature. Many Chinese restaurants in China, as well as other parts of the world, serve this dish, but usually with less authentic flavor compared to that found in Hangzhou, capital of Zhejiang Province, which has unique access to the fish and water from West Lake.

Every Dish Has a Story

The names of Chinese dishes are diverse, but behind each of the famous dishes is an interesting story explaining why it is popular. A catchy name may add value to the dish. However, some names are so eccentric that they may confuse people, both Chinese and foreigners. If you explain the names in a literal way, you may make a fool of yourself.

Take Goubuli steamed buns in the city of Tianjin for example. These popular buns are all handmade and of the same size. When served in neat rows in the tray, they look like budding chrysanthemum flowers. The wrapping is thin, the fillings are juicy, and the taste is tender and delicious yet at all not greasy. Then why the name?

There is an interesting story behind it. Goubuli steamed buns were first sold in Tianjin about 150 years ago. A local young man by the name of Gouzi (Dog) worked as an apprentice in a shop selling *baozi* (steamed buns). Three years later, he set up his own *baozi* shop. Because his buns were so delicious, he soon had a thriving business, with more and more people coming for the buns. As hardworking as Dog was, he still could not meet the demands of his customers, who had to wait a long time. Impatiently, some people would call out to urge him on, but as he was busy preparing the buns, he had no time to answer. People therefore called his buns *Goubuli*, meaning "Dog pays no attention." This eccentric name, however, had very good promotional effects, and has been used ever since. Now Goubuli is a time-cherished brand name in Tianjin.

In Zhejiang cuisine, there is a well-accepted dish called Dongpo Meat. This dish is prepared over a slow fire, with streaky pork in big chunks and garnishes of green onion, ginger at the bottom of the pot, cooking wine, soy sauce, and sugar. The finished dish is bright red in color and tender and juicy in taste, yet without any feel of greasiness. This dish was named after Su Dongpo (1037-1101), a great poet of the Northern Song Dynasty (960-1127), who created it when he was an official in Hangzhou. It is said that, when he was in charge of the drainage work for the West Lake, Su Dongpo rewarded workers with stewed pork in soy sauce, and people later named it Dongpo Meat, to commemorate this gifted and generous poet.

Fujian cuisine boasts a famous dish called Buddha Jumping the Wall, the No. 1 dish of the province. This dish is prepared with more than 20 main ingredients, including chicken, duck, sea cucumber, dried scallop, tendon, shark lip, fish maw, ham, and more than a dozen garnishes like mushrooms, winter bamboo shoots and pigeon eggs. All these ingredients are placed into a ceramic pot, with cooking wine and chicken broth added, and then cooked over a slow fire until the meat is tender and juicy and the soup becomes smooth and thick. A taste of the dish will leave a lingering aftertaste in the mouth. The story behind the name of the specialty goes thus:

This dish was created by a restaurant called Gathering Spring Garden in Fuzhou, Fujian, during the reign of Qing Emperor Guangxu (r. 1875-1908), first named Eight Treasures Stewed in a Pot and later changed to Blessing and Longevity. One day, several scholars came to Gathering Spring Garden for a drink. When the dish was served, one of them improvised a poem: "*Fragrance spreads to the neighborhood once the lid lifts, / One whiff and the Buddha jumps the wall, abandoning the Zen precepts*," hence the name of the dish.

Pale green glazed container, Yuan Dynasty

Warmth and Hospitality Expressed by Food

In the West, a separate meal for each person has been the practice since ancient times. Even at a banquet, people take what they like for themselves rather than sharing dishes. With ever-widening opening up to the outside world, this Western culinary practice has exerted a certain influence on China, yet has not basically changed the eating habits of the Chinese people. In the eyes of the Chinese, what is important about eating, especially at festivals, is to eat in a certain atmosphere and with certain sentiments. In the process, the old and young sit in order of seniority, talking and laughing in a joyous atmosphere, where the elders select food for the young, and the young make toasts to the elders. It is a lively, warm and harmonious family reunion.

Glazed plate shaped like a chrysanthemum flower, Yongzheng reign (1723-1735), Qing Dynasty

A hostess or host in China would apportion the dishes to treat guests. Using a pair of serving chopsticks, she or he offers the best part of a steamed fish to the most important guest. Such customs of arranging dishes are still popular among elder Chinese, as a way of expressing respect, concern and hospitality.

Such culinary customs have had a certain influence on the character of the Chinese people. In a sense, it has strengthened the collective spirit of the nation. At a party or a banquet, everyone first takes into consideration the needs of the group; with the eating process also being a time to show humility and concern for others. This is different from Western eating habits, which pay more attention to individual needs.

In China, people are particularly concerned with what foods to eat during festivals. At different festivals, people partake of different fare. For example, on the eve of the Spring Festival, people in the north choose *jiaozi*, meat and vegetable dumplings, at family reunion – bidding farewell to the old year and welcoming the New Year. The Lantern Festival is a day of celebration, and on this day people choose to eat *yuanxiao*, sweet dumplings made of glutinous rice flour, to symbolize family reunion and perfection. At the Duanwu Festival, people eat *zongzi*, glutinous rice wrapped in reed leaves in a triangular shape, to commemorate the beloved poet Qu Yuan (c. 339-c.278 BC), who drowned himself in the Miluo River after being politically wronged. Legend has it that people at the time threw *zongzi* into the river in hopes that the water dragon would not take him away. This later gradually developed into the custom of making and eating *zongzi* for the Duanwu Festival.

Superb Skills of Chinese Chefs

Chinese cooking attaches symbolic importance to the idea of making dishes by hand, and this is one reason for the quality of the cooking. Sometimes, eating is like enjoying an acrobatic performance. For example, pared fresh noodles, a specialty of Shanxi Province, are made in an acrobatic style. A cook stands a meter away from a wok, in which water is boiling. With a chunk of dough set on his arm and a sharp knife in his hand, he pares the dough into thin pieces projected right into the boiling water, a scene very much resembling fish diving into water. Any person witnessing this scene for the first time would be fascinated by the superb skill of the cook, so much so as to forget to eat. It is even more interesting to know that in the past a cook usually put the dough on his head and used two knives instead of one to pare the noodles. That would have looked even more like acrobatics than a cooking method!

Sichuan *dandan* noodles, much like the pared noodles of Shanxi, are a staple for ordinary people. *Dandan* noodles are cleverly prepared, with a specially concocted sauce of sesame oil, chili pepper oil, Chinese prickly ash oil, mustard oil, garlic oil, fennel oil, and chicken oil, in addition to the tender tips of pea vines, chopped green onions, and bean-sprouts. *Dandan* noodles used to be sold by vendors who wielded wooden clappers to attract customers. On hearing the familiar sound, people would gather around the vendors. All those served would nod their appreciation. Some people remark that the cooking wisdom of the Sichuan people has been concentrated into one bowl of *dandan* noodles.

Chinese people are very particular about the color, aroma, taste, and form of culinary dishes. For example, Beijing roast duck prepared by Quanjude Restaurant has well reflected these four aspects. As a celebrated dish with a history of nearly 150 years, Beijing roast duck is now world-famous.

Preparing quality roast duck involves a long, complicated process of many steps, from selecting the duck at the beginning to serving it to the diners at the end. Each step is carefully executed to guarantee the roast duck is shiny in appearance, jujube red in color, aromatic, and hot with thin steam when served. In the restaurant, ducks are roasted upon the order of diners. After a roast duck is ready, it is put on a big plate on a buffet cart and brought to the diners, in front of whom a chef will skillfully slice the tender, juicy meat, each piece with crispy skin attached. Dipping the slices of duck into sweet sauce made of fermented flour, the meat is then wrapped with some scallions inside a thin pancake, and only then does one finally take a bite! The remaining bones of the duck are stewed for making delicious, cream-white soup. If you go to a restaurant with friends who enjoy having a drink, the duck's wings, feet, heart, and liver, etc., all go well with wine, thus making the dinner an unforgettable "full-duck banquet."

27. Life with Fragrant Tea

Tea is a wonderful beverage originally produced in China about 4,000 years ago. During the Tang Dynasty (618-907), Japanese monks introduced tea seeds to Japan, and by combining tea with Zen Buddhism, created the world-famous Japanese tea ceremony. In the 17th century, the Dutch took to Europe the Chinese habit of tea drinking, which then became a tradition of the Europeans. In England in particular, people developed the custom of afternoon tea. Prior to the 19th century, all the tea in the world was grown in China, and even the English word "tea" was a transliteration of the pronunciation of "tea" in the Fujian dialect of China. Tea is an important contribution of the Chinese people to the world.

In China, the home of tea, drinking tea is still a widespread habit. Over the past several thousand years, tea has been the most favored drink of the Chinese people. As vast a country as China is, the tea-drinking habit varies from north to south in style, and different tea-drinking habits have helped develop different local customs. Tea is closely related to the everyday life of ordinary people.

Just as many important events took place in cafés in the West, it is in the teahouses that many important things happened in China. Teahouses have always been an important setting in the life of the Chinese people.

Magical Functions of Tea

When tea was first introduced to Europe, it was warmly accepted and even acclaimed as a "blessing from God," and people went so far as to congratulate themselves on being alive at such a time when tea leaves were found. In China, love for tea is just as, if not more, ardent.

Liu Zhenliang, a tea master of the late Tang Dynasty, whose birth and death years are unknown, once put forward the theory of the "ten virtues" of tea: tea is tasty; tea can maintain health; tea can drive away stinking odors; tea can prevent the attack of diseases; tea can cultivate energy in the human body; tea can relieve depression; tea can improve manners; tea can convey respect; tea can soothe the mind; and tea can uphold justice. This was not merely the personal view of Liu Zhenliang, but ideas shared by a majority of the Chinese people.

Seal carving, by Huang Yi (1744-1802), Qing Dynasty: inscribed with a line of verse expressing the relaxed mind while drinking tea.

Drinking tea is to satisfy the needs of the body as well as the mind. A cup of refreshing tea is able to naturally relieve a person of thirst while giving comfort and pleasure. According to traditional Chinese medicine, drinking tea can cure a variety of diseases, because the slightly bitter and astringent tea contains elements salutary for the body. This has been proven by modern medicine. Chinese people are fond of tea because it helps to satisfy their physical and, more, spiritual needs. The Chinese also use tea to express respect, to purify the mind, and to better perceive the meaning of life.

To tea drinkers, the first and foremost pleasure derived from drinking tea is "cleansing." Tea prefers to grow in clean places. The cleaner a place, the better the quality of the tea it nurtures. Fine teas usually grow on high mountains, enveloped in clouds and mists and in a clear atmosphere. In such an environment, transparent new tea leaves grow and are picked with the dew still clinging to them, hence the tea leaves carry the refreshing air of nature. A cup of fine tea is crystal clear and refreshingly fragrant, so that it can help the body become cleansed and balanced.

The second important facet is that of "seeking leisure." The bustling world, full of confusion and argument, weariness and exhaustion, damages the mind and body of human beings. A cup of refreshing tea can parry the sound and fury of the secular world at arm's length. In the process of sipping tea, the mind may

Lu Yu Making Tea, by Zhao Yuan (birth and death dates unknown), Yuan Dynasty. Lu Yu (733-804) of the Tang Dynasty was the acclaimed Tea Saint of China.

Boccaro teapot, produced in Yixing during Emperor Yongzheng's reign (1723-1735)

become as calm as a lake on a windless deep night when the moon shines brightly illuminating the world. A cup of tea may open up a new, boundless world.

The third important feature is that of "paying respect." The Chinese people have long fostered the custom of expressing respect by presenting a cup of tea. They treat guests with tea as a sign of respect, regardless of whether they are thirsty or not, and guests drinking the tea feel refreshed and energized. Educated people treat their guests arriving at night with tea instead of wine, a practice highly appreciated by the literati. In some places in China, there is the custom of presenting tea three times to the guests, as a sign of welcome, then of hospitality, and finally for good wishes. Presenting tea to guests demonstrates not only hospitality but also one's respect for the guests.

Ways of Savoring Tea

The Chinese people look to tea drinking as an art, which incorporates a wide range of knowledge; the taste of tea might be light, yet the meaning is rich and deep.

The Chinese attach great importance to the water, tea leaves, tea set, and fire, when making and drinking tea.

Water is an element of priority in the making of tea. To make a good cup of tea, quality water is a must. The ancient Chinese commented on tea making thus: the tea must be new, and the water must be live, or flowing. Lu Yu (733-804), Tea Saint of the Tang Dynasty, pointed out that, to make fine tea, water from high mountains is best, followed by water from rivers and wells. In the cloud-enveloped high mountains, crystal clear spring water is the best for making tea; water in the brooks though also good, is not pure because it smells of the earth, therefore is only second best. Considered third is water from wells, as artificial springs from underground are often stagnant and tinted with the flavor of salt. It is thus no match at all for uncontaminated mountain spring water. Unluckily for us today, we do not even have the third type of water to make tea; we use either tap water or artificially purified water – a true pity indeed!

The Chinese people also like to collect snow to make tea. The leisurely scene of "making tea with freshly collected snow, while reading in the light of a lamp on a cold winter day," is admired by many literati. Snow is white but easily contaminated, therefore people like to collect fresh snow to make tea.

Baotu Spring, acclaimed "No. 1 Spring under Heaven"

As making good tea needs good water, Chinese people have long developed the tradition of valuing springs, while springs have become famous because of people's love for tea. It is said that Lu Yu had traveled around the country, tasting different types of water in different places. He finally came to the conclusion that the Huishan Spring in Wuxi, Jiangsu Province, was the best for tea; the Baotu Spring in Ji'nan, Shandong Province, was second best; and the Hupao Spring in Hangzhou of Zhejiang Province, came third.

After water, the second most important factor for making good tea is tea leaves. China has a long history of cultivating miscellaneous tea leaves. From the perspective of processing, tea leaves fall into the categories of green tea, black tea, oolong tea, dark tea, and scented tea. Green tea is the main type of tea, and its output encompasses about 70 percent of total production each year. The famous green teas are Longjing of Hangzhou, Biluochun of Jiangsu, and Huangshan Maofeng and Liu'an Guapian of Anhui. Black tea is fermented tea, the most famous being Qimen Black Tea of Anhui and Dian Black Tea of Yunnan. Oolong tea is mainly produced in Taiwan and in the Wuyi Mountains in Fujian. Dark tea is represented by Pu'er Tea of Yunnan. Dark tea is processed by adding water to dried green tea leaves, which are then fermented. There are a variety of scented teas, including chrysanthemum and jasmine tea, the favorite of northern Chinese.

Fine tea needs to be served in a fine tea set. The Chinese people pay particular attention to tea sets, which may be made of porcelain, ceramic, glass or wood. China, since it is the home of porcelain, provides a solid foundation for research into making quality porcelain tea sets, though the tea sets the Chinese use are not necessarily porcelain ones. Instead, ceramic tea sets are gems in the eyes of tea lovers. One typical representative is the boccaro tea set produced in Yixing near Taihu Lake in Jiangsu Province, which has long been popular with people in both ancient and modern China.

The fourth and final element in making good tea is the fire, which should be, first of all, "live," as evidenced in the verse by the famous Song-dynasty (960-1279) poet Su Dongpo (1037-1101): "Flowing water needs a live fire." A "live fire" refers to a charcoal fire. Second, the fire should be slow, and a charcoal fire meets this requirement, as charcoal lights more slowly than other fuels do. Moreover, charcoal exudes a sense of the wild while not having that reek of smoke abhorred by tea lovers.

In the Chinese tea ceremony, there are four tenets that a tea drinker should observe, i.e., color, aroma, taste, and form.

First, observe the color. Different teas have different colors, such as black tea, green tea, oolong tea, white tea (leaves with fine and soft white hair), and dark tea. When making tea, people have different color requirements for these different teas.

Green tea should be fresh, and the best green tea is produced in spring. Tea picked either before Qingming Festival or the Grain Rain (day marking the beginning of the sixth solar term that falls on April 19, 20, or 21), is favored by people, due to the leaves' tenderness, freshness and greenness with a touch of yellow. This type of tea presents an unforgettable transparent image in a glass of hot water. Oolong tea has a deep brown color giving a sense of weight and seclusion. It should be made in a teapot, and look thick and golden when poured in a teacup.

Two boccaro teapots, Qing Dynasty

Second, observe the aroma. Fine tea should have a special fragrance of its own. The Chinese people have three ways of enjoying the aroma of tea: smelling it with one's nose once the tea leaves are put into a teacup; tasting it with the tongue once the tea is in the mouth and the fragrance overflows; and appreciating it with the heart as the unforgettable aroma lingers in the mouth, just like enjoying a fresh breeze.

Third, observe the taste. Mention the taste of tea, and a tea lover would tell you that the bitterness of tea is the most important of all tea flavors. Tea itself has a subtle bitterness, which, if one sips it slowly, would turn into sweetness, that is, when bitterness ends, sweetness begins.

Fourth, observe the form. The shape of tea leaves should also be observed when drinking tea, especially green tea. For example, the tender leaves of Longjing Tea, picked in the mists, would each stand up in hot water before they slowly unfold and stretch and fall down. Against the background of a white teacup, they look as if they are performing a graceful dance. Liu'an Guapian, another famous green tea, is another good example. The edge of each leaf of this kind of tea curves upward, its color bright green. In hot water, the leaves resemble lotus flowers, hence the tea has long been a favorite of Chinese people.

A scene of a "Tea Appreciation Ceremony" in the Lao She Teahouse in Beijing

Fine tea is a combination of color, aroma, taste, and form, and requires patience to be well appreciated. Therefore, Chinese people speak of "savoring tea," instead of "drinking tea"; any hurry here would be taboo.

Tea Drinking and Folk Customs

Drinking tea, a long-established custom popular with the Chinese people, is closely related to their life in a myriad of ways. It can not only refresh the mind but also add a poetic quality to life.

Wang Zengqi (1920-1997), a contemporary Chinese writer, once recalled his student years in the Southwest Union University in Kunming and remembered one poem on the wall of a teahouse near the university:

In those good times of old,
To a teahouse my father I followed.
Before the teahouse I played with shells
And at the lane entrance, with sand.

Wang Zengqi believed this was "a truly fine poem." The author describes the ritual of following his father to a teahouse during his childhood. He played with shells and sand at the entrance to the lane in front of the teahouse. What a happy time it was! The whole poem expresses a soft, touching melancholy permeated with strong poetic flavor.

Many Chinese folk customs are related to tea, such as the wedding ceremony. Tea trees grow out of seeds, and cannot be moved, so newlyweds customarily plant tea seeds to symbolize their devotion to love. The engagement ceremony is called a "tea ceremony" in China, which is still popular in some places.

Many love songs are related to tea drinking, too. According to the records of Lu You (1125-1210), a Song-dynasty poet, in some places, single young men and women often met to sing: "*Young girl, as pretty as tea leaves, / Would you please come out for a cup of tea?"* The song compares a beautiful girl to refreshing tea leaves, while the wooer expresses his love for the girl by inviting her to tea.

Tea drinking, with the touch of love, can be very romantic, along with its strong aesthetic elements. In the collection of short stories entitled *Strange Tales from Make-do Studio* (*Liaozhai zhiyi*), by Qing-dynasty (1616-1911) writer Pu Songling (1640-1715), there is a story telling of the love of Wang Gui'an and Yunniang. When the young man Wang Gui'an visits Yunniang's home in a dream, he witnesses a scene of "a silk tree in full bloom," as described in the following folksong:

My home is situated by the Pantuo River,
Come have tea some time, my sweetheart.
With earthen walls and a thatched roof,
In front, a silk tree in full bloom.

The silk tree and drinking tea both symbolize love and marriage. With these two images, this romantic love song sounds even more vivid and poetic.

28. Civil Residences in Deep Alleys

China is a country of vast territory with many distinctive local customs, leading to the emergence of a rich range of folk architectural styles. Here we will discuss four architectural styles: the *siheyuan*, or courtyard in Beijing, the ancient town of Lijiang in Yunnan, the folk residences in the mountains of Anhui Province, and the ancient town of Xitang south of the lower Yangtze River. Each has its own unique characteristics, while at the same time well reflecting the Chinese style of civil residences.

Siheyuan in Beijing

The courtyard architectural style exists in both southern and northern China. The courtyards of Yunnan in southern China are famous for the elegance of their white walls, black tiles, colorful paintings, and stone and brick carvings, in addition to lush green foliage. Courtyards in the north are represented by the *siheyuan* in Beijing, a symbol of the city.

The outstanding feature of a Beijing *siheyuan* is the "yard," a closed space formed by four rows of houses on its four sides, with only one gate leading to the outside world. If there are windows facing outside, they exist only on the southern wall of the southern house and high above the ground. It makes for a completely secluded world, once the gate is closed.

As the main style of civil residence in Beijing, the *siheyuan* first appeared in the Yuan Dynasty (1206-1368), when Beijing became the capital city. In the urban design of the time, civil residences were required to be built in a courtyard style, in which connected courtyards formed the alleys and blocks. Though each unit was independent, these courtyards formed an organic part of the city landscape.

The closed courtyard style was inherited by later generations because it well suited the geographic characteristics of the area. Beijing, as a large city and a transport hub, had a large population of migrant people. Safety was an important

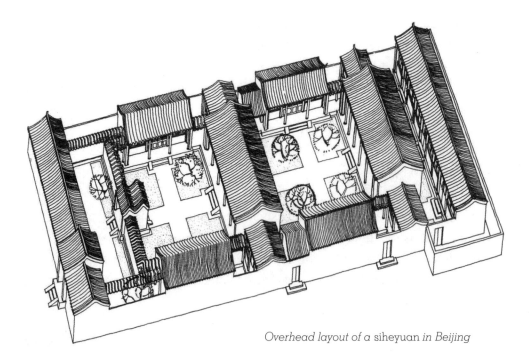

Overhead layout of a siheyuan *in Beijing*

Chuihua *gate in a*
siheyuan

factor that had to be taken into consideration. And the courtyard, with its high strong walls, locked gates and high windows, well served this purpose.

Beijing is a city that frequently endured sandstorms in the spring and icy cold winds in the winter. The limited number of windows of a courtyard prevented the sand from invading, while keeping the bone-biting cold air and wind outside. Today, many *siheyuans* have been torn down, and their residents have moved into high-rises. However, at night when cold winds roar, people often miss the peace of the courtyard, which once served as a haven for their ancestors.

Though closed, a *siheyuan* is a compact world. Once inside the courtyard, there is a screen, behind which is the *chuihua* gate, or the inner gate that has a decorative roof with short carved posts hanging down from the four corners. This inner gate leads to a yard, the center of the courtyard. Opposite the inner gate is the main house, flanked by a row of rooms on each side. All the doors of the rooms open into the yard. Inside the yard can be found goldfish tanks and different kinds of plants and flowers, such as plum and date trees, Chinese flowering crabapple, pomegranate, oleander, and Chinese wisteria. Residents can thus appreciate flowers in the spring, have shade in the summer and harvest in autumn – "not a day without something fine to enjoy all year round," as contemporary Chinese writer Yu Dafu (1895-1945) once remarked.

The courtyard was not only a world of fragrant flowers and lively creatures, but also a harmonious world of a huge family. A *siheyuan* usually belonged to one family of several generations. They would live in different rooms according to seniority, respecting, loving and caring for each other. Whether the outside world was turbulent or not, the inside always had spring sunshine, warmth and love, a peaceful, comfortable sanctuary for family members.

Later, different families moved into one courtyard; however, its advantages were not lost. The family atmosphere still remained and would touch the hearts of all residents, who, like one big family, supported and cared for each other. This family atmosphere is cherished in the memory of all those who once lived in a *siheyuan*.

Siheyuans in Beijing are also highly valuable in artistic terms. The gate of each courtyard is artistically accomplished, with carvings and paintings. Such artwork, along with the stone piers that support the pivot of the gate, all demonstrate Chinese craftsmen's unique management of space and color. The *chuihua* gate's carved posts hanging down from the four corners and the carved stone piers on the ground present a dignified splendor. The screen opposite the gate is a place to give flight to the imagination, and upon which there are always novel brick carvings. People appreciate *siheyuans* because each is a world of art that adds significance to their lives.

The feature of a *siheyuan* most worthy of admiration is that each and every one of its details manifest the idea of its harmonious existence with nature. Facing toward the south, a *siheyuan* enjoys ample sunshine in winter and refreshing cool in summer. The house in the north is the most important locale, enjoying the best energy of the courtyard. The gate opens southeast instead of being on the axis line of the compound. To enter into the yard, one needs to walk around the screen; thus passersby outside cannot witness the activities inside. Moreover, the screen prevents the wind from directly blowing in when the gate is opened, as well as adding diversity to the strict layout of the courtyard. Corridors inside connect all the rooms and give shelter to the residents on rainy or snowy days. As the southern exposure of a house usually takes in a great deal of heat in summer, a *siheyuan*, usually consisting of three yards in a row, is usually designed narrow east and west and long north and south, to reduce the chance of exposure to the sun.

Siheyuan is the creative product of human beings taking careful consideration of the "character" of nature, and making full use of its favors. It is a good example of harmonious coexistence between humans and nature.

Ancient Town of Lijiang

"The place the sun first shines upon is Jiantang in the east, and the most beautiful place in the human world is Shangri-la by the Naizi River." This is a folk song of the Tibetan people describing the beautiful landscape in Yunnan. Shangri-la was originally a fictional place depicted in the 1933 novel *Lost Horizon* by British writer James Hilton (1900-1954). It is a permanently happy land, isolated from the outside world. Today, Shangri-la has become synonymous with any earthly paradise. The Shangri-la of the Tibetan folksong is a land of peace, with high snowcapped mountains, undulating forests, shining lakes, cattle and sheep grazing and frolicking on vast pasturelands, and with golden temples glimmering amidst white snow.

Resembling this haven of peace and nestled at the foot of snowcapped Yulong Mountain is the ancient town of Lijiang, which was built in the later half of the 13th century. More than 600 years have passed, yet the city is still in fine shape, home to generations of Naxi, Tibetan, Bai, Yi and Han people.

A serene scene in Lijiang

The ancient town of Lijiang is as beautiful as Yulong Mountain, and as mysterious and peaceful as Shangri-la. Shangri-la, in Tibetan language, means "the sun and moon of the heart;" and this ancient town is indeed the sun and moon within the heart of the Naxi people.

Harmony between humans and nature was the lofty pursuit of the developers of this ancient town. Surrounded on three sides by high mountains, the town is home to several thousand households. All the houses face south to receive the blessings of sunshine from nature. Residents here plant trees along the streets and flowers at home. If you walk around this ancient, tranquil town on an early summer morning, you find the refreshing fragrance of flowers in every corner of the place.

Unlike other towns, this ancient town has neither wide streets nor a strictly planned layout; everything seems to come from nature, free and unaffected. The town spreads outward without painstakingly pursuing a predestined order. Like unencumbered vines climbing upward, it develops freely in response only to the power of nature.

The water system in Lijiang also expresses such freedom. The town's existence depends on water, while the water flows through or around the town wherever necessary. Northeast of Lijiang is the Black Dragon Pool, which gathers the water of melted snows from the high mountains, and then distributes it to every lane and every house along the narrow streets. Streets and lanes meander side by side along the brooks, with houses built over the water, so each household has water flowing past their home. There are nearly a thousand bridges of different sizes and types: arched stone bridges, level bridges, bridges for horse-drawn carts, bridges with carvings, and bridges over very narrow waters that people could actually stride over. The last type, of narrow bridge, though seemingly of

A small bridge in the ancient town of Lijiang

no practical use, was built at appropriate places, thus adding idyllic interest to the surrounding scenery.

Sifang Street is the center of ancient Lijiang, actually a square small in size. Many streets start here and spread in all directions, and are then connected to many lanes. The town resembles a huge leaf, with streets like veins along limpid brooks extending endlessly forward. All the streets radiating from the center are paved with colorful stones.

"Three houses in a row and one screen" is used to describe the features of the civil residences of the Naxi people. Residences here are also in the courtyard style. Once inside there is a screen; then the main rooms for the older generation, which face south; and lower than the main rooms are the rooms on the east and west, where the younger generation live. The yard is usually paved with bricks and stones, with unpaved spaces left for growing flowers and plants. There are usually flying eaves, and the roof is in the shape of steep slopes, which adds liveliness to the strict architectural style.

Flying eaves of an ancient temple in Lijiang, Yunnan Province

Civil residences in Lijiang usually consist of a back courtyard and a front courtyard, or of courtyards standing side by side, thus achieving a sense of spaciousness. The climate here is very pleasant all year round, so there is usually a patio attached, an open place for taking rests, having meals and receiving guests.

White Walls and Black Tiles, Anhui

In southern Anhui Province, civil residential complexes with white walls and black tiles dot the green fields and lush mountains. Acclaimed as living folk arts museums, these residences are outstanding symbols of villages and residences south of the lower Yangtze River. They may not appear so interesting at first glance, yet once you enter you experience the special beauty of simplicity and purity exemplified by this white and black world. Their profiles are lightly outlined against a background of green mountains and limpid waters; the white sands on the islets of the rivers extending and intermingling with the green in the distance; with streaks of looming mountains enveloped in clouds further away – all making for an idyllic, effervescent world.

The remaining traditional residences today in southern Anhui Province were all built during the Ming (1368-1644) and Qing (1616-1911) dynasties, with special attention paid to their unique architectural style, strict layout and abundance of carvings. There are now 45 well-preserved ancient villages, as well as a large number of valuable ancient houses in more than 7,000 sites. Residences in Xidi, Hongcun and Chengkan villages have combined to form a vast folk arts museum in the Huizhou style.

Xidi, acclaimed as the earliest village of Huizhou-style residences, is an ancient community constructed by the Hu family. One of the important buildings here is Lufu Hall, built in 1691, with very refined carvings. Inside the hall, the furnishings are warm, gracious and exquisite. The hall exudes a strong scholarly flavor, as suggested by its hanging couplets exhorting people to study hard, remain filial, and work diligently. The whole ambience displays the owner's adherence to Confucianism.

A residential hall in Huizhou, Anhui Province

Walking through the deep and serene alleys is a great pleasure. The alleys are stone-paved, flanked by high and erect white gables, or horse-head-shaped wall tops, as special structures and features of the Huizhou-style residences. A village here is usually home to generations of families with the same surname. As the housing density is high, and most of the houses are built of wood, gables are specially built high to prevent the pread of any fire that might break out. The gables are much higher than the walls of the houses and uneven in height, yet evoke a sense of momentum as if in flight. This sense of mobility adds vibrancy to the crowded and closed village. Standing on higher ground, one gets a panoramic view of the whole village: the white gables rising high in midair looking vitally powerful.

The *tianjing*, or patio, is another feature of a Huizhou-style residence, which usually consists of two courtyards: one being outside the residence, and the other inside. The inner yard, or *tianjing* as locals call it, can collect both water and energy according to Huizhou people, and is thus regarded as a symbol of accumulating fortune. Therefore, rich families attached great importance to the construction of the inner yard when they built the houses. The inner yard is formed of the walls and eaves of surrounding houses, like a funnel; thus rain and melted snow fall into the yard. This inner yard is a haven for the residents, who grow flowers, enjoy fish in aquariums and listen to the rain here.

A water system is very important in residential areas, and especially so for these Huizhou-style residences, which were usually built at the foot of mountains. Diverting springs from the high mountains to each household is how Huizhou people have solved the problem of drinking water. Hongcun Village, listed as a world cultural heritage site, is famous for its special water system. There are several hundred families living in this village, which has a layout in the shape of an ox – agriculture and oxen being closely related in China. Water flows down from the mountains behind the village, and meanders along streams through stone bridges and to each household, and finally into the Moon Pool. After being filtered in the pool, the water again flows on, out of the village to the low-lying South Lake. The streams here symbolize the intestines of an ox, with the pool as the stomach, and the lake as the belly. This is an interesting design for a water system.

Xitang, a Serene Water World

Civil residences south of the lower reaches of the Yangtze River are famous for their fresh and elegant styles and distinctive features. The ancient town of Xitang is a typical example of these dwellings.

Xitang is located in Jiaxing, Zhejiang Province, between Shanghai and Hangzhou. Though small in size, this ancient town boasts a long history. It was first built in the Spring and Autumn Period (770-476 BC), at the border between the states of Wu and Yue. The present layout had already taken shape before the Song Dynasty (960-1279), and the famous Wangxian Bridge in Xitang is a legacy of the Song. By the Ming and Qing dynasties, Xitang had become a renowned trade center for farm products, silks and ceramics, all produced in the surrounding areas and famous throughout the country.

The residences in Xitang are built alongside the water. "Families live in the midst of waters, bridges arch over the rivers, passengers walk across the bridges, boats pass under the bridges; shops stand at the head of bridges, and their reflections sway in the water," is how people described the village. A newcomer strolling through the town is soon plunged into a real-life intoxicating landscape painting.

Xitang is situated on the shores of Taihu Lake, with the Great Canal passing by it. There are nine winding rivers intersecting the town into eight blocks. Each house is located facing a river, as are the shops. Xitang people row small boats along the rivers to their destinations, instead of walking on foot through streets and lanes. Weeping willows and colorful flowers grow along the riverbanks, and flocks of water birds and white geese play on the water dotted with plants of floatingheart. Several hundred ancient bridges of different shapes and sizes arch over the rivers like crescent moons. Famous bridges include the Wufu, Wolong, Huanxiu, and Songzilaifeng bridges. Walking on the bridges is like walking along streets of the heavens.

One feature of the houses in Xitang is their seclusion and serenity. As land is limited, Xitang people make careful calculations when they build houses and lanes. All the 100-plus lanes are less than one meter wide but more than 100 meters long. Standing in such a lane and looking upward, one only sees a line of sky overhead; walking on the stone-paved lanes, one's echoing steps make the ancient lanes appear even more mysterious and secluded. The most famous lane is Stone Skin Lane – so named because it is paved with thin and shiny slabs of stone. Along Stone Skin Lane are its two most famous buildings – Zhongfu Hall and Zunwen Hall.

The serenity and seclusion of Xitang is also reflected in the depth of the house, a Chinese aesthetic ideal in the construction of a residence, as evident in the verse line, "How actually deep is the deep compound?" Many rich families built residences with several courtyards in a row. Three courtyards in a row is commonplace; while a large residential compound has five or seven courtyards.

A scene south of the lower Yangtze River

Zhongfu Hall, mentioned earlier, has seven courtyards: the first is the entrance hall with high gates, carved beams and painted ridgepoles; the second is for sedan-chairs; the third is the main hall, called Zhongfu Hall; the fourth, for flowers; the fifth, the living quarters; the sixth and seventh, respectively, for the granary and hired staff. With a garden rearmost, this compound extends more than 100 meters long. Such an architectural style explored the essence of "depth" to the extreme.

29. Martial Arts and Cuju

Traditionally, the Chinese love sports as an essential method for keeping fit as well as for entertainment, like the dragon-boat races during the Duanwu Festival, swings at the Qingming Festival, and climbing mountains during the Double-ninth Festival. People also relate sports to an enhanced insight into life, such as with go and Chinese chess. As a country with diverse cultural traditions passed down from one generation to another over a long history, China has developed a variety of sports, including archery, *cuju* (traditional football), sumo and other forms of wrestling, equestrianism, martial arts, and acrobatics. Among these, martial arts and acrobatics may be said to be the "superb" skills of China.

Martial Arts of the Shaolin Temple

When people talk of the martial arts, or kung fu, they most immediately think of Bruce Lee (1940-1973), and his great accomplishments in boxing, swordplay, and skill with knives and sticks. With his superb kung fu popularized throughout the world, he became the embodiment of Chinese martial arts. His dazzling three-section stick skills left a deep impression on audiences. Bruce Lee's kung fu was deeply rooted in traditional Chinese martial arts.

In Chinese martial arts circles, Shaolin Temple enjoys great repute for its distinct style of martial arts – a precious feature of China's cultural legacy. Shaolin Temple, located on Songshan Mountain in Henan Province, was first built at the end of the fifth century. Bodhidharma, a Buddhist master, came here in the sixth century, and through meditating by facing a wall for nine years developed Zen Buddhism (known as "Chan" in China), hence making the temple famous throughout the country. Later generations attributed the invention of Shaolin martial arts to him, saying that due to long periods of sitting, he created a set of movements to adjust the internal circulation of the *qi*, or *chi*, and relax the body and mind. Shaolin martial arts have developed a variety of forms over the long years, hence the attribution of "72 types of Shaolin martial arts." Long boxing, short boxing, knife and stick play and swordplay, each claims its own unique skills. Shaolin Temple has had a far-reaching influence on Chinese martial arts.

Shaolin children's kung fu is a superb skill highly acclaimed by martial arts practitioners. This martial art includes many movements and postures, such as "arhat sleeping," "child worshipping Guanyin," "child worshipping Buddha," etc. Children's kung fu is a relatively difficult type of Shaolin boxing that needs complex training from childhood.

In Shaolin boxing, there is one movement known as "One-finger Zen," considered one of the secrets of Shaolin. It is said that the key to this martial art lies in inner discipline, which condenses and focuses all one's energy and strength onto one finger, so that the practitioner is able to stand upside down on that single finger, absolutely still.

Arhat boxing is one of the many types of boxing created by the Shaolin Temple. It has been developed into several sets of movements, gaining far-reaching influence across the country. This set of boxing, exquisitely designed and easy for attack and defense, is powerful and unpredictable. It has long been regarded as "the best of the best" in Shaolin martial arts.

Shaolin martial arts stress training in the basics. Today, a visitor to the Shaolin Temple can still see the shallow holes on the ground left by generations of martial arts practitioners in the One Thousand Buddha Hall. It is their sweat and wisdom that has carried on the splendid tradition of Shaolin martial arts.

Flowing Shadow Boxing

As one of the main sports to help people stay fit, *taiji quan*, or shadow boxing (known internationally as "tai chi chuan") is very popular with Chinese people. It used to be a martial art, but since it aids both self-defense and health, it quickly developed to become a main method of physical exercise. Shadow boxing can adjust the neural, respiratory, digestive, coronary, brain, and circulatory systems of the human body, functioning as a method for disease prevention.

"Taiji" (the Supreme Ultimate) is a Chinese philosophical term, to which *The Book of Changes* (*Yijing*) attributes the origin of the Eight Trigrams. *Explanation of the Taiji Diagram* (*Taiji tushuo*), written by Northern Song (960-1127) philosopher Zhou Dunyi (1017-1073), regards Taiji as the source of all things on Earth. The Taiji is circular in shape, including the *yin* and the *yang*, and shadow boxing was created exactly on the basis of this theory.

Being "circular" is one of the important characteristics of shadow boxing. Performing shadow boxing is just like drawing circles again and again, while being smooth and round is a major criterion in judging the quality of its performance. Heaven and Earth have energy circulating around them, while inside a human body circulates the vitality of life. Shadow boxing draws the circle of life through moving, jumping, dodging, unfolding, etc., so as to turn exterior circles of energy into interior circles of energy. Another characteristic of shadow boxing is its pursuit of flowing rhythm amidst the changes of *yin* and *yang*, which accords with the Taiji philosophy that *yin* and *yang* interchange, infuse and change. On this basis, shadow boxing emphasizes the infusion of the hard and the soft, and expresses the constant changes of the universe through gentle and flexible, and even and slow movements. In general, shadow boxing displays the beauty of soaring clouds and flowing waters.

In the course of its development, shadow boxing has incorporated the theory of main and collateral channels in traditional Chinese medicine, along with the idea of guidance advocated by Daoism. Shadow boxing is a combination of the interior and the exterior, and people practice it to improve physical health and to achieve evenness in breathing and calmness in mind. When practicing shadow boxing, one needs to pay particular attention to breathing air out through the mouth when making outward movements and inhaling fresh air through the nose when making inward movements, so as to keep fresh energy in the body. This is why people prefer to practice it in the early morning.

Shadow boxing and Shaolin martial arts both have deep and profound philosophical connotations; they embody the unique wisdom of the Chinese people, and reflect the identity of Chinese culture.

Martial Arts from the Heart

Controlling mobility with stillness is one of the characteristics of Chinese martial arts. For example, shadow boxing gives off a sense of elegance and quietude, while emphasizing changes in tranquility. When practicing shadow boxing, the practitioner first straightens the body, closes the eyes, keeps energy in check, lets the hands naturally down, and expels all worry and disturbance before starting to practice. Shadow boxing stresses the training of even breathing and a serene mind, but "the momentum of shadow boxing is like the ocean, surging forward without cease," as people note. Under the peaceful surface are the wild ocean currents, yet a tolerant heart embraces all things on Earth.

Dynamic Shaolin martial arts also emphasize the combination of motion and stillness, as described in the words of a song: "*Lie like a bow, stand like a pine tree, sit like a bell, and walk like the wind.*" The highest criterion for Shaolin martial arts is the oneness of movements and Zen Buddhism, through which one is able to achieve the goal of quietly practicing Buddhism. Before practicing martial arts, the practitioner must first sit in quietude on a rush cushion, achieve calm, focus energy, and only then slowly stand up free of any worldly cares. Shaolin martial arts, described as "coming from emptiness or soulessness," places emphasis on the training of the mind and on combining mobility with tranquility.

Defeating the strong with the soft is another important feature of Chinese martial arts. For example, Shaolin martial arts require a practitioner to jump, land, advance, retreat, turn aside, etc., in a straight line, with the purpose of collecting energy inside rather than of keeping the body steady; and once in attack mode, one directly hits the vital parts of a rival at the fastest speed and with the greatest strength imaginable. Some people describe Shaolin martial arts as being "elegant like a cat, yet fierce like a tiger; walking like a dragon, moving like lightning, with a voice like thunder." Shadow boxing, though lacking a single distinctive line, has a seemingly broken line linking the flow of energy. Shadow boxing, also called "lithe hands" or "cotton circles," is a gentle art, like a languid, enchanting dance, starting slowly and ending slowly, as naturally as if no force were applied. However, practitioners have the ability to launch a sudden attack to effectively defend themselves. Therefore people compare shadow boxing to water – gentle but powerful.

Generally speaking, Chinese martial arts are a type of defensive martial arts, where offensive attack is not the main goal. The three purposes of Shaolin martial arts are to protect the temple, protect oneself and keep fit, rather than to attack others. Resorting to force only when there is no alternative is one characteristic of Chinese martial arts, as well as a feature of military theories in China. One commandment of the Shaolin Temple is the requirement to "hold morals in esteem, rather than force," as evidenced by its incorporating the concept of "benevolence" in Confucianism and by its principle against brutal attack. Shaolin martial arts stipulate the "eight don'ts" when one has to resort to force: don't attack the temples, don't attack the chest, don't attack the soft ribs, don't attack the armpits, don't attack the private parts, don't attack either side of the small of the back, don't attack the coccyx, and don't attack the auricles. These body parts are delicate, and the regulation of the "eight don'ts" is to avoid taking life.

Cuju Flew Higher than Birds

Cuju, or *cuqiu*, meaning "kick ball," is a type of ancient Chinese football. *Cuju* was already called "football" during the Song Dynasty (960-1279), as evidenced in *Collection of Xikun Songs* (*Xikun chouchang ji*), a book by Yang Yi (974-1020), which contains the following line: "*Cuju* uses the feet to kick the ball, hence called 'football' today."

A Scene of *Cuju*, by Qian Xuan (1239-1301), Yuan Dynasty. It depicts the founder of the Song Dynasty, Zhao Kuangyin (r. 960-976), and his ministers playing cuju.

Many ancient Chinese paintings depict scenes of *cuju*. One painting, *Longevity and One Hundred Children*, by Song-dynasty artist Su Hancheng (1094-1172), features a scene of a group of children playing *cuju* together. One child is lifting his foot to kick a ball. Another painting, entitled *A Scene of Cuju*, by Qian Xuan (c. 1239-1299), of the early Yuan Dynasty (1271-1368), describes Song Emperor Taizu, or Zhao Kuangyin (r. 960-976), playing *cuju* with five of his ministers. The six players are depicted vying with each other to kick the ball, when even the emperor momentarily forgets his identity, enjoying himself in high spirits like everyone else.

Cuju is said to have first appeared in the ancient era of the Yellow Emperor. Liu Xiang (c. 77-6 BC) of the Han Dynasty (206 BC-AD 220) recorded in his *Miscellanies* (*Bielu*): "*Cuju* is said to have been invented by the Yellow Emperor, or during the Warring States Period. It was originally a method to train soldiers, and through *cuju*, soldiers of talent can be found. For enjoyment, soldiers like to play it when they are free from duty." It might not be true that *cuju* was first developed in the time of the Yellow Emperor, but historical documents record clearly that this sport was quite popular in the State of Qi during the Warring States Period (475-221 BC). This sport was originally popular in the army, as a type of activity involving both conflict and entertainment. The military thus discovered soldiers with ability while they exercised their bodies through the sport, which also would have slightly relieved the boredom and loneliness of barrack life.

In the Han Dynasty, the sport of *cuju* became very popular. Huan Tan (? BC - AD 56), said in his *On Salt and Iron* (*Yantie lun*): "Noble families engage in *cuju* and cockfighting." The court field for *cuju* was a rectangle, while the ball was round, which accorded with the Chinese idea of "the sky is round and the land is square." A closed space within high walls, the court field had stands specially built for distinguished spectators. "The Ball and the Court Field," an essay written by Li You (birth and death dates unknown) of the Eastern Han Dynasty (25-220) and inscribed on the cornerstone of a court, records that the game was usually played between two teams, each having 12 players in the field, with goals on both sides, as well as referees. No specific rules for the game are known today. According to *Miscellanies of the Western Capital* (*Xijing zaji*), after Liu Bang (r. 206-195 BC), founding emperor of the Han Dynasty, ascended the throne, he made arrangements for his father to live in Weiyang Palace, providing him with delicacies as well as song and dance performances. However, the old man remained in low spirits. It turned out that Liu Bang's father had lived with ordinary people and liked to indulge in cockfighting and ball-playing. Upon learning the truth, Liu Bang had a new town built with a large *cuju* court in honor of his father, who then invited all his old friends, and from then on led a very happy life.

Tang-dynasty mirror featuring a polo match

The football used in the Han Dynasty was already made of leather, but filled with solid materials instead of air. The Tang Dynasty (618-907) witnessed the invention of the air-filled ball, which made the sport more interesting, as this ball was elastic and could fly high into the sky. Tang-dynasty people paid great attention to the atmosphere of the matches, beating drums to add to the fun. However, the level of confrontation was lessened, with the goals, earlier placed on the two sides, then put in the center of the court. But the entertainment was increased as people had to count the number of goals to decide who would win. Air-filled balls being light, people found another way to play with it, that is, to see who could kick the ball higher.

Cuju helped to develop another sport in the Tang Dynasty, polo. Polo appeared first in the Three Kingdoms Period (220-280); later as exchanges with the Western Regions increased, the polo of those regions found its way to China, enriching the sport. The popularity of the *cuju* game also enhanced the popularity of polo. In the Tang Dynasty, a polo match was once held between a Tubo (today's Tibet) team and a Tang team. Moreover, among the 19 emperors of the Tang Dynasty, 11 were fond of playing polo. Inside and outside the capital city of Chang'an, there were more than a dozen polo courts. Polo, besides being a form of entertainment, was also applied to train armies; and as a result, many cities and towns where troops were stationed had polo courts, too. In the tunnel of the Tomb of Crown Prince Zhanghuai (Li Xian, 652-684), the mural *Hitting the Ball* vividly depicts a scene of polo game in the Tang Dynasty.

The urban cultural prosperity of the Song Dynasty brought further popularity for *cuju*, with the entertainment aspect of the game highly increased. The Song people compared football with theater, and there even arose organizations like today's football associations. People loved *cuju*, and a good *cuju* player enjoyed high social status. In the novel *Outlaws of the Marsh* (*Shuihu zhuan*), there is an official named Gao Qiu, a real figure in history who was highly appreciated by Song Emperor Huizong (r. 1101-1125), simply because he was good at playing *cuju*.

During the Tang Dynasty, *cuju* became a popular folk activity played on "Cold Food Day," the day right before the Qingming Festival. Many poets of the Tang and Song dynasties composed poems describing scenes of playing *cuju*, as well as about the swings, thus giving us intriguing portrayals of these folk customs.

Women began to take part in the *cuju* game in the Tang Dynasty. By the Yuan Dynasty, there were already female *cuju* professionals. Yuan playwright Guan Hanqing (?-c.1300) had two poems under the same title "Women Xiaowei," describing scenes of women playing *cuju*. "Xiaowei" was a title for the highest-ranking craftspeople in the Qiyun Society a *cuju* association. They not only put on solo *cuju* performances, but also took part in man-woman competitive performances. This is depicted in two bronze mirrors with a *cuju* design, one now kept in the Museum of Chinese History and the other in the Hunan Museum.

Pottery polo players,
Tang Dynasty

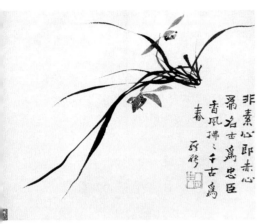

30. Go: a Game of Wits

Go is an important board game with origins in China from more than 4,000 years ago. It was introduced to the Korean peninsula and Japan over 1,000 years ago, and has since become a favorite pastime of many people there. Today, go still serves as a means of cultural exchange between the peoples of China, Japan and Korea, as they engage in numerous tournaments every year.

Go is not only a competitive event but also a game of entertainment. In the old days, literati would usually have a set of go pieces on their desks. When a friend came around, both host and guest would enjoy a game of go, along with fine wine, as described in the following lines of poetry: *"Enjoy a pot of fragrant tea till sunset, / Play a game of go till year-end."* In countryside and towns of old, a pair of go players in an open space would often attract an attentive crowd, with the onlookers enjoying the game no less than the players.

A Game on Rotted Ax-handle Mountain

There is a legend about the great allure of go. Wang Zhi, a Jin-dynasty (265-420) woodman, was on his way up a mountain to gather firewood, when he came across two fellows playing a game of go. He stopped to watch them and forgot all about the firewood. In the middle of the game, one of the players told him: "You should be going home. Look, the handle of your axe has rotted away." Wang Zhi hurried down the mountain, but when he arrived home, he could find none of his family there any longer. All the villagers, too, were strangers to him. Only an old well assured him it was indeed his home village.

This story is the source of an ancient Chinese saying: "Seven days in the mountains are as long as a thousand years in the world." In Quzhou, Zhejiang Province, there is indeed a Rotted Ax-Handle Mountain, said to be the location of the legend. "Rotted ax-handle" was later adopted as another name for the game of go. High-level go players sometimes write the Chinese characters 烂柯 (rotted ax-handle) on folding fans, and give them as gifts to lower-level friends.

Playing go helps to calm the mind. On a clear day, one can play a game with a visiting friend, while indulging in random reflections on life and history. Or, on a moonlit night, two friends might sit by a go board, while sipping cups of fragrant tea. Except for the moonlight shining through the window, nothing else seems to exist. Gone from their minds, too, are any thoughts of worldly favor or humiliation.

Traditional New Year painting. The two ladies to the right are preparing for a game of go.

Wisdom at Play

A game of go has many implications for real life. It is for the appreciation of such inferences that go appeals to both players and onlookers.

Go represents "a square world of round pieces in black and white." There are 181 black pieces and 180 white pieces. The square board and round pieces make up the world of go. While the board is fixed, the pieces can be placed in millions upon millions of different ways, just as life in the world may take many turns.

The go board has 19 horizontal and 19 vertical lines crisscrossing each other, forming 361 intersections, which are believed to be a replication of the days in a year. The round dots on nine of the intersections are said to represent the stars in the sky.

A go game may provide many lessons on life: hesitate when one has all the advantages, make a bold move when already under attack from all sides, complacent when success is just around the corner, over-anxious about gain or loss, or press an opponent too hard, all leads to failure. Master go players often feel as if they were playing a real-life game: sometimes one can forge forward, while at other times, one must slow down; sometimes one can directly face the opponent, at other times one must take an indirect route. Appropriate placement of each tiny go piece is similar to how one might solve a difficult problem in life.

A Game of Peace

Go players have beautiful names for the pieces: "crow" for the black pieces, and "gull" for the white ones. They are placed upon the board like birds alighting on a riverside. The use of bird names in go indicates that it is a poetic game, rather than a confrontational one.

In a game of go, the players do not "slay" each other's pieces. Instead, they simply try to win a larger share of space, allowing the other side some space,

Illustration from the classic novel A Dream of Red Mansions (Hongloumeng), *by Cao Xueqin (c. 1724 - c. 1763), Qing Dynasty. Playing go is a favorite pastime of the story's aristocratic female characters.*

too. At the end of a game, both sides have plenty of space on the board. The winner, of course, has the larger part, but the difference can be as tiny as the space for a quarter of a go piece. In chess and Chinese chess, on the other hand, the players try to "slay" as many as possible the other side's pieces. The one who forces the other side's commander into a dead corner then wins the game.

Go emphasizes peaceful competition and coexistence, whereas chess and Chinese chess stress a confrontational rivalry with a win-or-lose outcome. Therefore, although Chinese chess is also a popular game in China, go carries deeper cultural and philosophical implications.

The purpose of playing go is not just to win but also, and more importantly, to seek wisdom through the process. Winning or losing is only temporary. No one can be always victorious.

There is a prevalent saying regarding go: "Mere contention for victory does not a good game make." This illustrates a core concept of Chinese philosophy – non-contention, as advocated by Zhuangzi (369-286 BC). When criticizing the logician Huizi (c. 370-310 BC) for being good only at argument, Zhuangzi said, "It is meaningless to win an argument." Wisdom does not come out of arguments.

The highest goal of go is to seek harmony. The players unite with each other on the board. Instead of fighting as enemies, they cooperate to play a good game. Thus go players should always keep their minds free from intention of confrontation. The real test for a good player is to transcend the idea of winning or losing. Su Dongpo (1037-1101), a poetic talent of the Northern Song Dynasty (960-1127), was also a great go player. He had this thought to share with fellow players: "It is a pleasure to win. It is a pleasure to lose, too." Wu Qingyuan (b. 1914), a contemporary Chinese go talent who emigrated to Japan and made a name there, regarded go as a game that "seeks a world of harmony."

Hand Conversations

In China, go is also referred to as "hand conversations," through which players communicate with each other. In other words, they "talk" through the placing of pieces on the board. The metaphor originated with Zhi Daolin (c. 314-366), a Buddhist master of the Jin Dynasty (265-420). While scholars of his time often indulged in philosophical debates on life and the universe, Zhi Daolin preferred to play go, which he believed was full of the hows and whys of life.

In general, go-player pairs are usually appreciative friends. Only well-matched players are able to inspire each other. This is why master players sometimes lament the lack of worthy "inoculators." Ma Xiaochun (b. 1964), an established contemporary go player, once said, "When I play with someone who is able to appreciate me, I experience silent pleasure through every piece."

Therefore when playing go, one invites not an opponent but a kindred friend. Starting with an empty, open board, the two deploy the pieces together. They must cooperate in order to play a good game, because one thoughtless move could spoil all the enjoyment. The philosophy of go is also a philosophy on competition in general, as well as a philosophy on life as a whole.

We hope you have enjoyed reading these concise introductions to Chinese culture, and will take any insights learned to further delve into special areas of interest. Like a small path in a Chinese garden that leads to myriad wider vistas, this book is a first step toward opening up to you the fascinating world of China's ancient and ever vibrant culture. Enjoy the continuing journey…

A Brief Chronology of Chinese History

夏 Xia Dynasty			2070-1600 BC
商 Shang Dynasty			1600-1046 BC
周 Zhou Dynasty			1046-256 BC
周 Zhou Dynasty	西周 Western Zhou Dynasty		1046-771 BC
	东周 Eastern Zhou Dynasty		770-256 BC
秦 Qin Dynasty			221-206 BC
汉 Han Dynasty			206 BC-AD 220
汉 Han Dynasty	西汉 Western Han Dynasty		206 BC-AD 25
	东汉 Eastern Han Dynasty		25-220
三国 Three Kingdoms			220-280
三国 Three Kingdoms	魏 Kingdom of Wei		220-265
	蜀 Kingdom of Shu		221-263
	吴 Kingdom of Wu		222-280
晋 Jin Dynasty			265-420
晋 Jin Dynasty	西晋 Western Jin Dynasty		265-317
	东晋 Eastern Jin Dynasty		317-420
南北朝 Southern and Northern Dynasties			420-589
南北朝 Southern and Northern Dynasty	南朝 Southern Dynasties		420-589
	南朝 Southern Dynasties	宋 Song Dynasty	420-479
		齐 Qi Dynasty	479-502
		梁 Liang Dynasty	502-557
		陈 Chen Dynasty	557-589
	北朝 Northern Dynasties		386-581

		北魏 Northern Wei Dynasty	386-534
南北朝 Southern and Northern Dynasty	北朝 Northern Dynasties	东魏 Eastern Wei Dynasty	534-550
		北齐 Northern Qi Dynasty	550-577
		西魏 Western Wei Dynasty	535-556
		北周 Northern Zhou Dynasty	557-581
隋 Sui Dynasty			581-618
唐 Tang Dynasty			618-907
五代 Five Dynasties			907-960
五代 Five Dynasties		后梁 Later Liang Dynasty	907-923
		后唐 Later Tang Dynasty	923-936
		后晋 Later Jin Dynasty	936-947
		后汉 Later Han Dynasty	947-950
		后周 Later Zhou Dynasty	951-960
宋 Song Dynasty			960-1279
宋 Song Dynasty		北宋 Northern Song Dynasty	960-1127
		南宋 Southern Song Dynasty	1127-1279
辽 Liao Dynasty			907-1125
金 Jin Dynasty			1115-1234
元 Yuan Dynasty			1206-1368
明 Ming Dynasty			1368-1644
清 Qing Dynasty			1616-1911
中华民国 Republic of China			1912-1949
中华人民共和国 People's Republic of China			Founded on October 1, 1949

Index of Persons

Index of Major Sights

English	Pinyin	Chinese	Page
Hall for Listening to the Rain	Tingyu Xuan	听雨轩	147
Hall for Preserving Harmony	Baohe Dian	保和殿	82
Hall of Central Harmony	Zhonghe Dian	中和殿	82
Hall of Earthly Tranquility	Kunning Gong	坤宁宫	82
Hall of Heavenly Purity	Qianqing Gong	乾清宫	82
Hall of Literary Glory	Wenhua Dian	文华殿	82
Hall of Military Eminence	Wuying Dian	武英殿	82
Hall of Prayer for Good Harvests	Qinian Dian	祈年殿	28-30
Hall of Supreme Harmony	Taihe Dian	太和殿	82, 84
Hall of Union and Peace	Jiaotai Gong	交泰宫	82
Harmony Garden	Xiequ Yuan	谐趣园	147
Imperial Family Shrine	Taimiao	太庙	81
Imperial State Shrine	Sheji Tan	社稷坛	81
Imperial Vault of Heaven	Huangqiongyu	皇穹宇	31
Jade Spring Mountain	Yuquan Shan	玉泉山	146
Joyous Longevity Hall	Leshou Tang	乐寿堂	144
Kunming Lake	Kunming Hu	昆明湖	144, 147
Liangyi Pavilion	Liangyi Ting	两宜亭	147
Liuyuan Garden	Liu Yuan	留园	142, 147
Longmen Grottoes	Longmen Shiku	龙门石窟	105, 109
Lotus and Wind Pavilion	Hefeng Simian Ting	荷风四面亭	147

English	Pinyin	Chinese	Page
Maijishan Grottoes	Maijishan Shiku	麦积山石窟	107, 108
Meridian Gate	Wu Men	午门	81
Mogao Grottoes	Mogao Ku	莫高窟	105, 106
Moon and Wind Pavilion	Yuedao-fenglai Ting	月到风来亭	147
Museum of Chinese History	Zhongguo Lishi Bowuguan	中国历史博物馆	93, 250
Palace Museum	Gugong Bowuyuan	故宫博物院	117, 135, 137, 138, 171
Prospect Hill	Jing Shan	景山	81, 83
Shangri-la	Xianggelila	香格里拉	231, 232
Shaolin Temple	Shaolin Si	少林寺	241-243, 245
Smoke and Rain Hall	Yanyu Lou	烟雨楼	147
Summer Palace	Yihe Yuan	颐和园	139, 140, 144-147
Sun Yat-sen Park	Zhongshan Gongyuan	中山公园	81
Temple for the Divine Cultivator	Xiannong Tan	先农坛	80
Temple of Ancestral Worship	Fengxian Si	奉先寺	109, 110
Temple of Heaven	Tiantan	天坛	27-31
Terracotta Army	Bingmayong	兵马俑	99, 103
Three-Treasure Study	Sanxi Tang	三希堂	117
Tiananmen Square	Tiananmen Guangchang	天安门广场	80
Tiger Hill Park	Huqiu Gongyuan	虎丘公园	147

English	Pinyin	Chinese	Page
Wangxian Bridge	Wangxian Qiao	望仙桥	237
Working People's Cultural Palace	Laodong Renmin Wenhuagong	劳动人民文化宫	81
Yulong Mountain	Yulong Xueshan	玉龙雪山	231
Yungang Grottoes	Yungang Shiku	云冈石窟	105
Zhuozheng Garden	Zhuozheng Yuan	拙政园	140